A Conspicuous Situation

How Newcastle's Lit & Phil arrived on W

Alison Menzies

"This building stands in a conspicuous situation nearly opposite the west end of Collingwood Street"

Metcalf Ross, 1841

'to diffuse a spirit favourable to knowledge and virtue'

Contents

Foreword and Introduction by Michael Chaplin

I became a member of the Lit and Phil when I was 15 or so, at the urging of my father. Sid had become a devoted member (and later its vice-president) when we moved to Newcastle in the late Fifties and was so keen for me to join a decade later he paid my subscription until I left university. His motive was to aid my education – and believe me, at that point it needed all the help it could get. I vividly remember my first visit: pushing through the double-doors, climbing up the switchback staircase and into the vast airy space of the library itself, full of light, learning and a pregnant sense of its own history. If only walls could talk, I thought . . .

With this splendid little volume, engagingly written and finely illustrated, my curiosity about the building of the Lit and Phil in the opening decades of the 19th century is finally satisfied. Established in 1793, the Society first met in the elegant Dispensary in Low Friar Street, then moved to the 'old Assembly Rooms' in Ridley Court off the Groat Market before its growing collection of books, scientific instruments and specimens of geology and natural history demanded a solution for the long-term.

The story of what happened next is full of twists and turns, with a rich complement of heroes including a benefactor called Dr Headlam, a 34-year-old builder from Corbridge called John Green who later designed many railway bridges in the North as well as the Lit and Phil, and a slippery villain in the form of the Society's President no less, Sir John Swinburne Bart of Capheaton.

It all makes for a splendid tale, researched and related so well by Alison Menzies, and I commend it to all friends far and wide of this jewel of our city, the dear old Lit and Phil.

Michael Chaplin
June 2022

Preface

These pages aren't the work of a scholar, they're the work of someone who enjoys piecing a story together. For the necessary pieces however, I'm indebted to the work of many scholars. The dedication of chroniclers, draughtsmen and antiquarians through centuries is awe-inspiring. Their faded records release forgotten details and insights that have the freshness of colours in a newly restored oil painting.

The story is of a building, the Grade 2* listed, neo-classical building of Newcastle's Literary and Philosophical Society. More particularly, it's the story of the trials and tussles of the hard-pressed committee whose aspirations forged the building between 1822 and 1825.

To erect the building took only a few years, but seven hundred years of history already connected the building to the land on which it stands. Those connections remain embedded in Lit & Phil heritage, and they form a natural introduction to the main narrative. So the story opens with fleeting snapshots from the early centuries. For the handful of years it then took to create the Lit & Phil's permanent home, the snapshots merge into a steady footage, doing justice to the unfolding sequence of events and allowing a view of the main rooms as they were completed.

The building's history inevitably intersects with the Society's history, as well as with the history of the town. In the interests of a single trajectory, those avenues had to remain largely unexplored here; but the titles in the sources list should point in helpful directions. All sources used, published and unpublished, are included in an appended list, and can mostly be tracked down in dim corners of the Lit & Phil.

Alison Menzies, Newcastle 2022

AD 122-1066

Scene-setting

A bridge, a wall, a fort

AD c.200, imagined in AD c.1850.

The bridge came first. Then the wall, marching west from the bridge for seventy odd miles until it met the sea. Then more wall eastwards from the bridge, four precautionary miles in case anyone tried fording the river downstream. In time came a “castrum”, a fort, on the precipitous cliff overlooking the bridge.

And so the Romans placed the first marks on the map of modern Newcastle.

In the course of the next several hundred years, the Roman era declined and Anglo-Saxons moved in. The warring kingdom of Northumbria emerged; early Christianity flung a network of monasteries across the region. It’s speculated that the Anglo-Saxon name “Munecaceastre” (Monkchester), recorded only in later mediaeval documentation, refers to a township which grew around a monastic community founded on the place of the Roman castrum. The existing evidence for such a town is too slender for any certainties.

From the seventh into the ninth century AD, monastic life flourished across Northumbria. Then plundering Danes and Vikings invaded, and the monks were dispersed. Over the next two hundred years most traces of their former presence vanished.

In October 1066, far away on Britain’s south coast a momentous landing took place.

1080 - 1300

Ancient Names

To secure their northern dominion, the Norman invaders built a castle of timber and earth over the site of the castrum. Norman scribes called it *novum castrum*, the new fort. Or sometimes *novum castellum*, the new castle. In 1159 a taxation scroll identified the "town" as *burgum novi castelli*, the borough of the new castle.

Records were kept in Latin for some centuries more, so we don't know how soon locals began to identify their home as 'Newcastle'.

But another familiar name would have been in use very early on. Over the centuries, the decaying Roman wall had provided a ready-laid western highway. Conveniently it also offered free building materials. There were dwellings along this street from the town's earliest days. It was the Vikings who introduced the word 'gat', meaning a passage. Westgate was a thoroughfare centuries before it was crossed by the fortified West Gate of a mediaeval wall.

Quite early in the 1100s a new name arrived on Westgate:

There was nothing new about the feudal practice of conferring land on worthy recipients both secular and ecclesiastical. Northumberland wasn't short of wealthy estates with which Northumbrian kings and earls would reward (or buy) loyalty. Norman kings redistributed these estates among safe Norman hands. One Norman lord found his hands generously filled.

Some time after 1100, Henry I, grandson of William the Conqueror, granted the Barony of Styford in Northumberland to his Normandy-born subject Walter de Bolbec, in return for the service of five knights and castle-guard at the new castle. Attached to the gift came a small plot on Westgate, a stone's throw from the castle. The site became known as Bolbec Hall.

For about two hundred years Bolbec Hall remained in the hands of Bolbec descendants. During that time, the mediaeval town evolved and flourished. New religious foundations multiplied. To the Bolbecs' west, the Hospital of St Mary the Virgin (the "West Spital") was established; later the Whitefriars settled to their south. And the fledgling town became a thriving commercial centre in need of a defensive town wall.

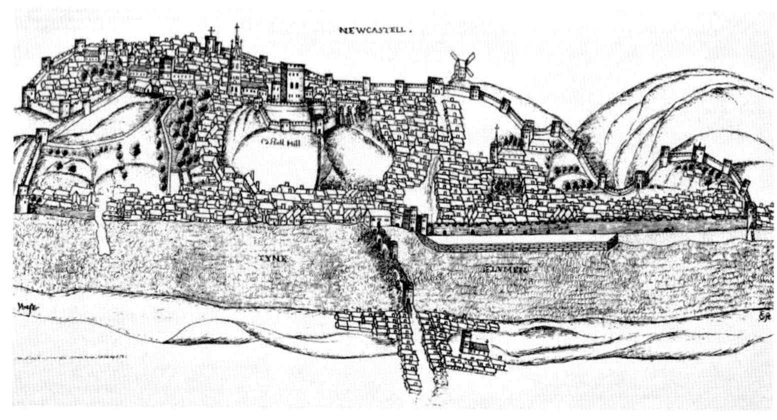

c.1545: walled Newcastle with twelfth and thirteenth century parish churches and friaries.

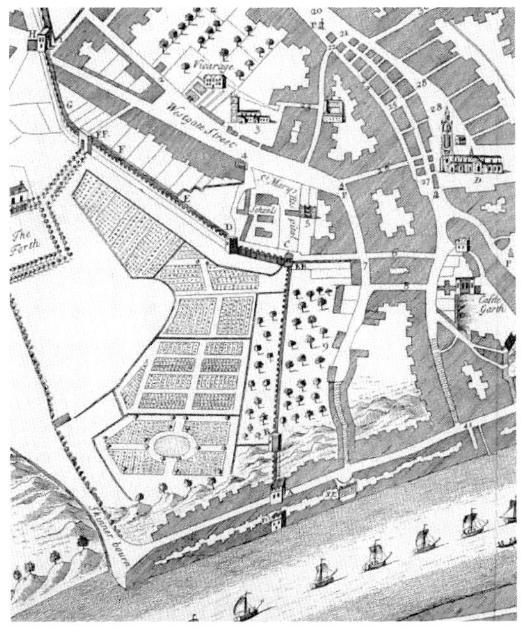

The building of the great wall was well under way in the 1300s, when the Bolbec property passed into the hands of another powerful northern family, the Nevilles. On course to join the castle, the wall curved south-east from its fortified West Gate past the southern boundary of the West Spital. Then there was a change of plan. In order to include riverside inhabitants within its protection, the wall turned through ninety degrees at the bottom of the Nevilles' garden, to drop sharply south towards the river. The tower built at the resulting corner, defending Neville property, was financed by the Nevilles and took their name.

The detail from Henry Bourne's map of 1736 shows the wall four hundred years after it was built. You'd expect to see crenellations on a defensive tower, but now Neville Tower has a pitched roof. This wasn't its original look. By Bourne's time, many of the wall towers had been adapted to serve as meeting halls for the town guilds. For the remainder of its existence, Neville Tower was characterised by its pitched roof.

The south-striding wall is shown cutting through the orchard which was previously the Whitefriars' garden. To allow the friars to access their land outside the wall, a formidable postern gate had been built into the corner. The woodcut print is an 1846 reconstruction of the corner's appearance "around 1600", seen from outside the wall looking east through the postern gate. The original Neville tower looms on the left.

By 1805 the gate had become an obstruction to traffic and the wall around it was demolished. The drawing below shows what remained in the 1840s. We're inside the wall now, looking in the opposite direction towards the gap where the gate had been. The pitched roof still identifies a much altered Neville tower, and a last remnant of the wall still stands. The tower was a familiar landmark until in 1847 it too succumbed to progress. It disappeared beneath railway tracks, to bequeath the name of Neville to the new street leading past the magnificent new Central Station.

1300-1820s

Snapshots

Westmorland House . . .

The photograph shows a section of mediaeval wall revealing the outline of an arch. Elsewhere in these walls, stone lintels can be seen - minus doorways or windows - inserted at haphazard levels in the masonry. The walls are a palimpsest of ancient building history. They're the existing walls of the Lit & Phil's cellar.

It would take removal of the structure above the cellar to investigate that history. But what's certain is that the age of this masonry connects back to Neville occupancy of the site. A deed dated 1370 refers to the property standing here as "the great mansion of Lord John De Nevill". Six and a half centuries ago, today's cellar could have been Lord John's ground floor.

Throughout the 1300s the Nevilles were a brutal superpower in Northumberland, condoned by monarchs for their useful suppression of northern insurrection. In 1397 Sir Ralph Neville was created the first Earl of Westmorland. Marking this aristocratic pinnacle, he renamed his great mansion "Westmorland House". No doubt he also made building alterations befitting his new status.

In the 1400s a fault-line appeared in the Neville power structure: Sir Ralph's second marriage gave rise to rival inheritors. Successors to the Earldom continued to be based in the traditional Neville seat at Raby Castle. They managed to preserve royal favour, and remained a force to reckon with. But the Nevilles pulled out of Newcastle.

Perhaps the Westmorland House name never stuck. At the time of Sir Ralph's death in 1425 a document is said to have referred to his house as "Neville's Inn". In 1486 another deed refers to the site merely as "the land late of Ralph Nevill, Earl of Westmorland".

In the 1500s, it was religious conflict which became the Nevilles' undoing. In 1569 the sixth Earl of Westmorland embraced the Catholic "Rising of the North" against Queen Elizabeth's Protestant monarchy. It didn't end well for Catholics. The upshot was that the entire Neville line forfeited its right to own property in England. Earls of Westmorland ceased to exist.

The deeds show that already in 1559 Lord John's "great mansion" was occupied by merchant tenants called Bartram. Now the Bartrams took the opportunity to purchase it. By now it was over 200 years old. And judging by the cellar walls pictured here, it was much patched.

Next door, change was afoot.

. . . and Westmorland Place

On the adjacent site now occupied by the Mining Institute building (in 2021 relaunched as The Common Room of the Great North) there stood another property of ancient origins. In 1608 it passed to a new owner. "Timothie Draper, of Newcastle, gent." had grand designs. The deeds tell the story. Between 1610 and 1613, the gentleman persuaded his merchant neighbours to sell him parcels of "waste ground" from their land, amounting to a substantial rectangle running back from the street. The Bartrams also consented to building plans potentially encroaching on the fabric of their property. The outcome was presumably the imposing wing to the street seen in T.M. Richardson's nineteenth century drawing. Apart from some restyled windows the house appears unaltered since its Jacobean makeover.

It might have been these developments which occasioned a curious wandering of the Westmorland name. Although now stripped of its aristocratic credentials, the name probably carried a seductively aristocratic ring. A little over a century after Timothie Draper's rebuild, the Reverend Henry Bourne made strenuous attempts to unearth the history of this corner of Westgate Street. Apparently the Westmorland name's historical connection with the Bartrams' side had dropped out of town memory. Bourne and his sources connected it only with the handsome Jacobean mansion next door, now widely known as Westmorland Place.

The slippage has caused much debate as to which is the original Neville site. Bourne's history of Newcastle, published posthumously in 1736, contained ambiguities which fuelled the argument. Bourne was well aware of the limitations of his work. According to the somewhat aggrieved Reverend, his researches had been compromised by social prejudice: for reasons of snobbery he was denied sight of essential documents. Prevented from getting to the bottom of contradictory anecdotes, he could offer no certainties. Appendix 1 has details of this story.

What was withheld from Bourne in the 1730s was granted in the 1890s to the antiquarian Richard Welford. All the deeds referred to above are cited by Welford in his illuminating article of 1898. They conclusively demonstrate that the so-called "Westmorland Place" site had no historical connection with the name of Neville. In his article Welford calls it the "sham" Westmorland Place.

So it's official! The Lit & Phil can justly claim the Neville and Bolbec pedigrees.

Des Res

In 1723 the young James Corbridge published a map he described as an "actual survey" of Newcastle. It records a town relishing its participation in modern urban life. The river is bustling with shipping, the town's trade guilds ("Companys") are foregrounded in a prominent section of the key, schools and charitable institutions are displayed, neatly tended gardens adorn almost every corner of town.

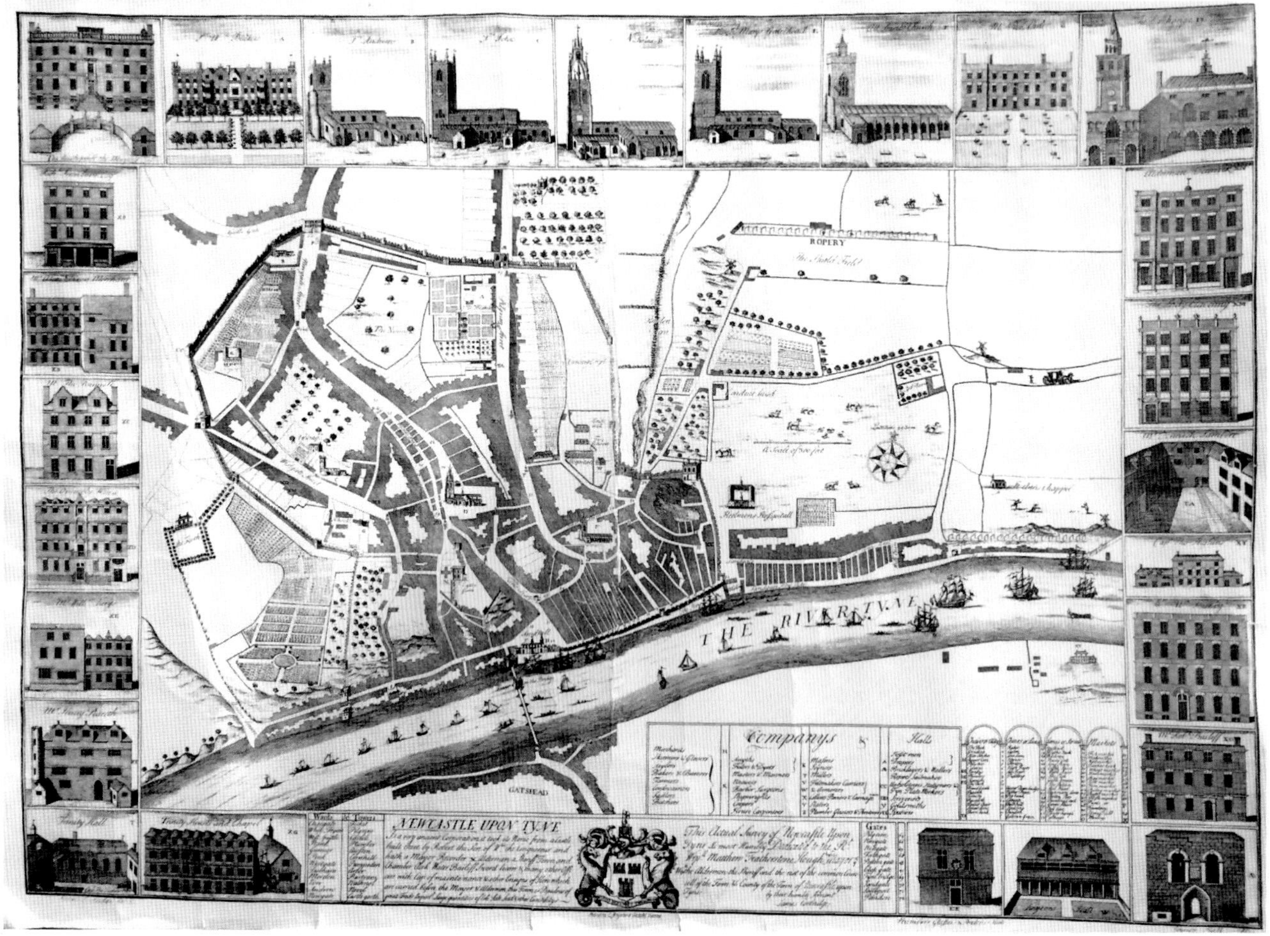

The map's border attests the gentry's fondness for their town houses. It showcases twenty-six individual buildings, among them a dozen private residences of named gentry. The inclusion of these twelve depended not on rank or merit, but on the standard commercial practice of subscription: Corbridge had advertised that those gentlemen who subscribed to his map project "shall have the Prospect of their Houses in the Margin". He might have hoped for more takers.

The two narrow plots which in 1723 were about to cause headaches to Rev. Bourne lie side by side just west of the bend of Westgate Street. Marked by the letter G, a new great mansion graces the former Neville site. It enjoys both its "Prospect in the Margin", and the distinction of a sketch in elevation on the map itself.

By now the property had been in Bartram hands for generations. It looks as if some time around 1700 they had done their own stylish upgrade. This is the new look in domestic architecture, the tall, narrow sash windows organising a symmetrical brick façade. Another façade shown in Corbridge's border, Alderman Fenwick's, had its windows remodelled in this style some time after 1695. Also common to both these façades are the classical parapet and the projecting end bays which lend a whiff of the country house.

The Bartrams now owned a fashionable town residence, but the name of the subscriber who secured its portrait in Corbridge's border isn't Bartram. In 1723, the Bartrams were letting the house to a Mr Thomas Orde. A few years later, they sold it to him.

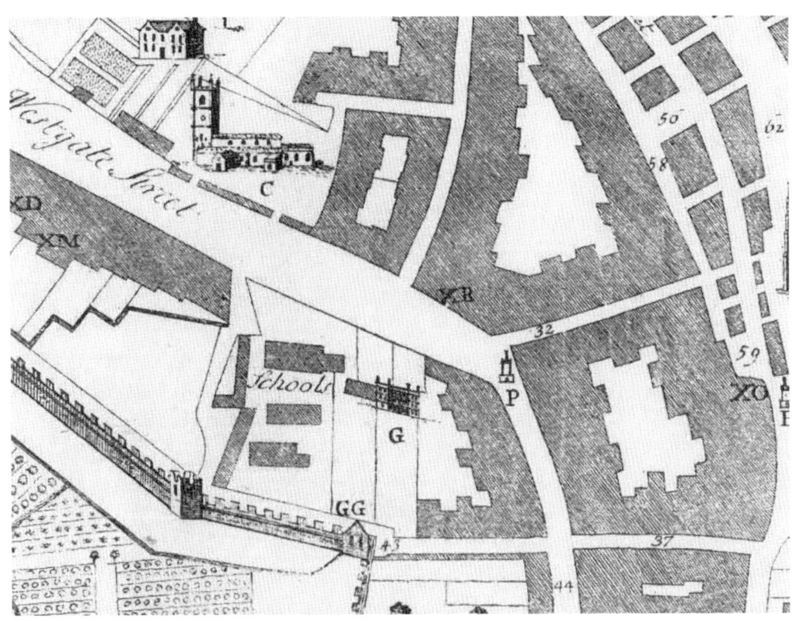

Corbridge isn't interested in superannuated mediaeval towers. The map key assigns to GG its contemporary status as the meeting hall of the "Bricklayers & Wallers, Ropers, Sailmakers". Bricklayers! Their standing must have been solid in a town where coal plentifully supplied bricks, and smart houses increasingly desired them.

The West Spital had lost its religious status after the Dissolution of the Monasteries. But its "Schools" were well-known. In 1723 not only the "Grammar School" but also simple reading and writing classes traditionally convened here.

The "sham" Westmorland Place, situated between the Schools and Mr Orde's, was approaching the end of nearly a century's ownership by the illustrious Shafto family. Corbridge represents the substantial dwelling with a humble rectangle. It can't have slipped through his surveying net. Someone didn't choose to subscribe.

In 1746, Isaac Thompson published his original map of Newcastle. No privilege here. Mr Orde's house is shown in simple ground plan, the long front garden open to the street just across from Denton Chare.

But Thompson does full surveyor's justice to the adjacent property. There's a lot more of it than of Mr Orde's. A major wing extends all the way to the street, even showing what's probably an accretion gained by the transaction with a Bartram in 1613. At the building's west end a small extension lends the ground plan a slightly hooked aspect.

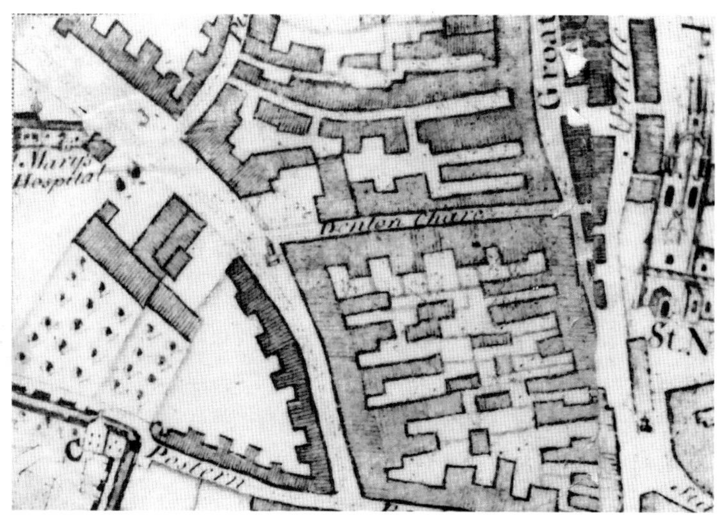

Detail from Thompson, 1746

Cartography made huge strides in the eighteenth century. The mathematician Charles Hutton surveyed a map in 1770 which presented the greatest level of accuracy yet achieved. Picture elevations have gone. The entire town is mapped in ground plan. The clearly recognisable hook shape of Mr Orde's neighbour shows a property detached from Mr Orde's house. The meticulous Hutton has drawn single lines in the Orde garden which might record the 1610/13 transactions encroaching on the garden's dimensions.

House and garden are entering their last half century.

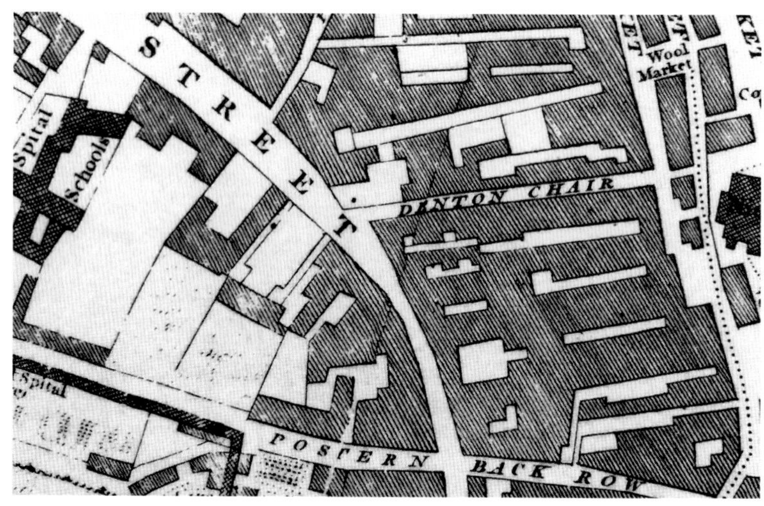

Detail from Hutton, 1770

Swan Song

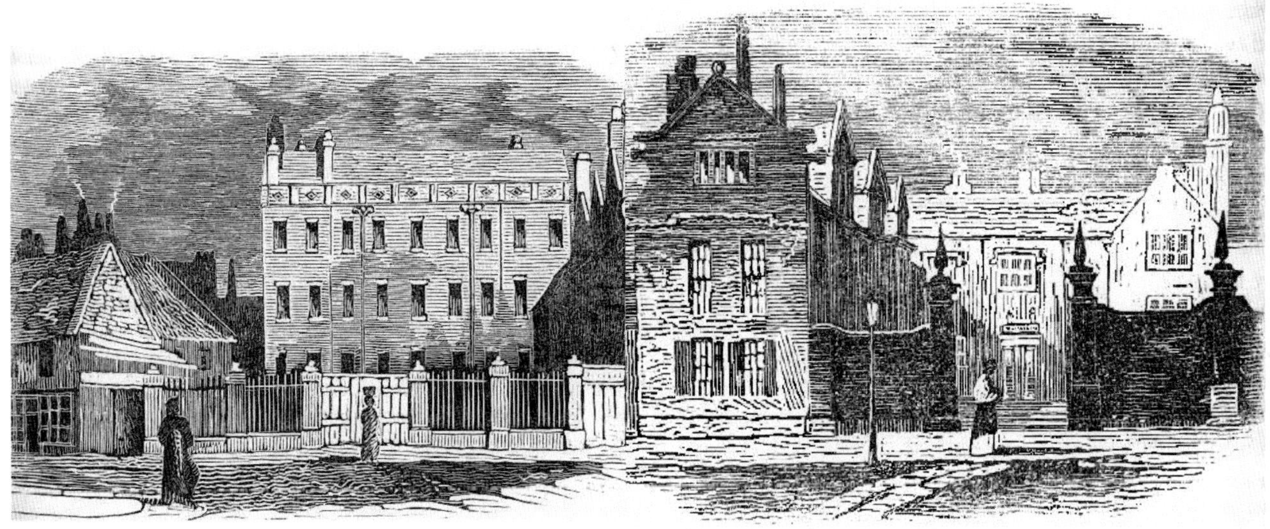

Westmoreland Place, Westgate Street, Newcastle. 1826.

Photography came a few decades too late to record the appearance of that little stretch of pavement. But we can juxtapose M.A.Richardson's two woodcut images from the 1820s to help reconstruct the scene in its final months. In reality the street bends away here, so the two fronts would turn slightly away from each other.

On the left is Mr Orde's house drawn in 1820. It looks as if an attic storey has been added since James Corbridge drew it. In deep afternoon shadow, a lean-to structure on the neighbour's great wing protrudes into Mr Orde's garden. But it's not Mr Orde's garden now: times have changed and the gentry no longer set store by fashionable town houses. The house has changed hands more than once recently and was last purchased by Mr Anderson. The boarded-up gates signal its altered fortunes. It's now in shared occupancy with Mr Angas, who will soon become its final owner.

In the adjacent drawing dated 1826, morning shadow darkens the west face of the neighbour's great wing. Through stately stone gateposts the mansion's porticoed entrance can be made out, set back from the street in the shelter of the "hook" of an extension projecting on the right. The building perfectly matches the hooked ground plan which Thompson and Hutton drew on their eighteenth century maps.

In 1826 the house is a grand age, but its Jacobean dignity is barely diminished. You can see why back in 1613 the gentleman Timothie Draper might have been tempted to appropriate the Westmorland name. Or was it Mark Shafto, esquire, future Recorder of Newcastle, when he took possession in 1642?

Westmorland Place managed to survive for another few decades after this drawing, long enough to appear in early photographs. But the days of Mr Orde's house are numbered.

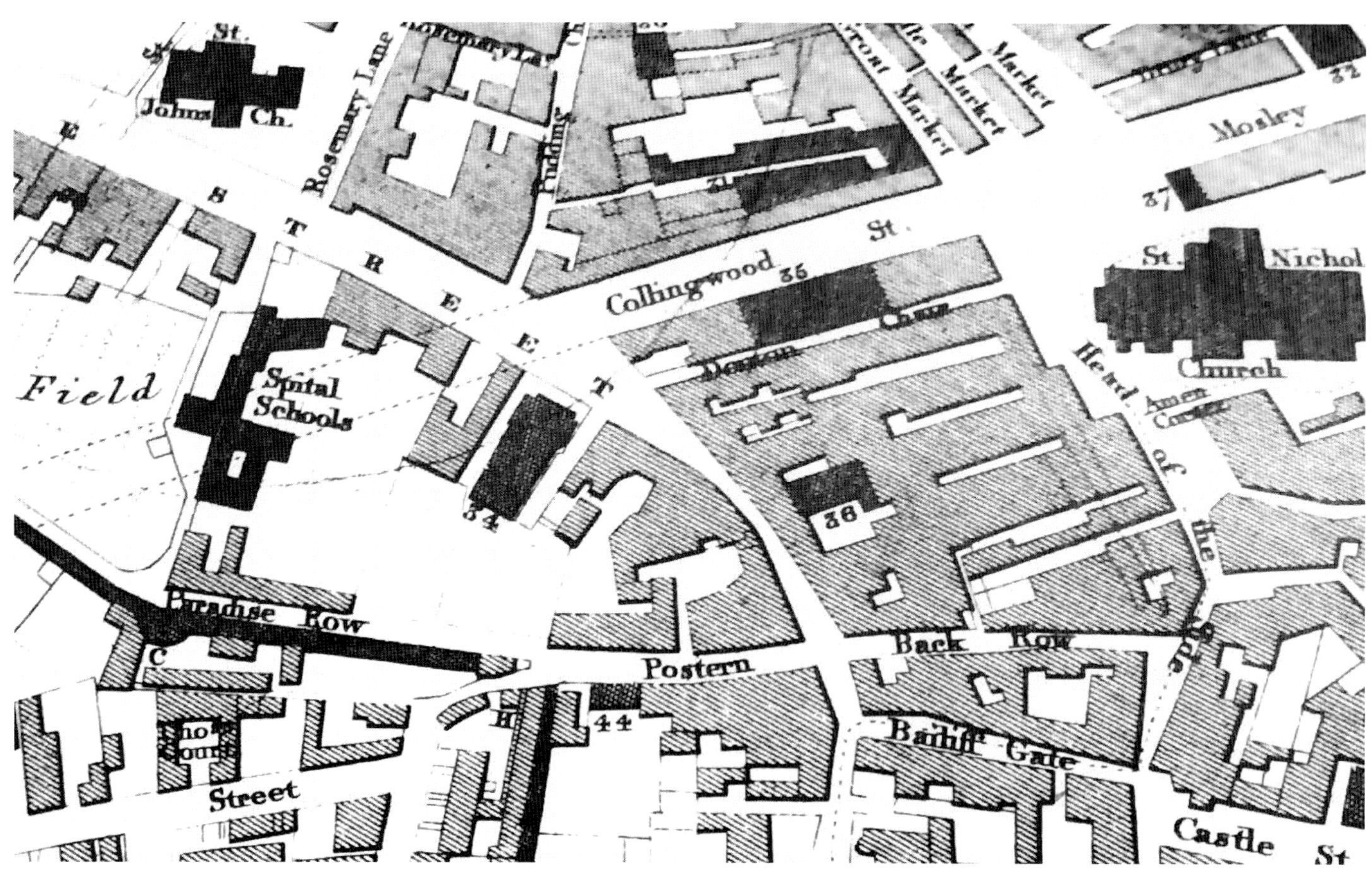

Finally, it has happened. John Wood's map of 1827 is the first to record the metamorphosis. Boldly high-lighted beside the hook of Westmorland Place, the newcomer takes its place among the town's significant public buildings. No. 34 in Wood's key is described as "Philosophical Society's Library".

1793-1822

Philosophical Society

Philosophical: loving wisdom!

It's scarcely possible for us to recapture the Enlightenment resonances of the word. It connoted optimism: belief in the power of knowledge, belief in human potential, belief in progress. And it denoted every kind of enquiry that pursued better understanding of the material world.

Today's equivalent term is "scientific". The new term with its rapidly evolving parameters began to replace the old from the 1830s.

Whichever word you used, if you were affected by the exciting developments of the times you needed to meet with like minds to discuss them. The old universities weren't an option. For one thing they excluded all religious "dissenters", many Northerners among them. For another, they purveyed a largely classical education. Even if university had been available to the general population, it hardly connected with the material world. Specially not with an industrial material world.

Then there was London's Royal Society. All fields of philosophical discovery and innovation were its domain. But London was far away and, be it admitted, the Royal Society membership was largely composed of swells.

The educated gentry of northern industrial towns were motivated not only by intellectual curiosity and generally liberal social attitudes: often they were hands-on practitioners with a personal stake in progress. In an age of societies, the obvious thing was to establish your own learned institution.

The meetings of the celebrated Lunar Circle of Birmingham had shown the way from 1765. In 1775 a small Newcastle group formed a "Philosophical Society", but it came to grief over radical politics. Credit for the first "Literary and Philosophical Society", with a benign social ethos and organised aims for the pursuit and promulgation of philosophical discovery, went to Manchester. In 1781 they inaugurated the model which in 1793 Newcastle emulated. These two remained the giants but by the time Wood's map was published, Literary and Philosophical Societies were recognised presences in several, mainly northern towns.

The indefatigable Unitarian minister William Turner was thirty-one when in January 1793 he delivered his "Speculations on the propriety of attempting the establishment of a Literary Society in Newcastle".

The New Institution

The Society's initial object had been to provide a regional forum for scientific and cultural exchange within its (predictably privileged) membership. But soon, informed by its Enlightenment roots, it reached out to a wider audience. In 1802, under the Society's patronage a "Lectureship on Subjects of Natural and Experimental Philosophy" was established. Through its annual programme of lectures the New Institution, as it was called, set out to open the expanding field of natural philosophy to less privileged members of society.

Tyne Mercury, November 11th, 1802

Permanent Lectureſhip

IN

NATURAL PHILOSOPHY, &c.

AT the ROOMS occupied by the LITERARY and PHILOSOPHICAL SOCIETY of Newcaſtle, (late the *Old Aſſembly Rooms*, in the Groat-Market) on TUESDAY the 16th inſt. the Rev. WILLIAM TURNER will deliver a

General Introductory Lecture,

On the Objects propoſed by the Society in the above-mentioned Inſtitution, the Advantages which may reaſonably be expected from it, the Nature of the Lectures which are intended to be given, and the probable Order of the ſeveral Courſes.

For the Accommodation of the different Claſſes of the Public, the Lecture will be given at TWELVE o'Clock, and repeated at SEVEN in the Evening.

TICKETS, Price 2s. 6d. may be had at the Library; at Meſſrs. Hodgſon's, Walker's, Brown's, and Mitchell's Printing-Offices; at Meſſrs. Charnley's, Akenhead's, Humble's, Bell's, and Sands's; at the Gateſhead Library; or of any of the Members of the Committee.—The whole of the Money received will be appropriated to the general Objects of the Inſtitution.

*** Donations and Subſcriptions, in Aid of the general Deſign, are received by Mr. BOYD, Treaſurer, at the Newcaſtle Bank; and by the LIBRARIAN, at the Rooms of the Literary and Philoſophical Society.

The Hedley Papers

The Society's early records are essentially scrapbooks: chunky volumes binding together collections of printed reports and articles, handwritten letters, announcements, newspaper cuttings, sketches and illustrations. One dedicated secretary, the Rev. Anthony Hedley, collated records in thirteen volumes spanning the first thirty-one years. A cutting from the Newcastle Chronicle records the gratifying success of the first lecture series.

Newc: Chron June 4th 1803

The first Course of Lectures, in the New Institution at the Literary and Philosophical Society's Room in this town, closed on Monday evening last. —The attention and liberal patronage of the public have equalled the most sanguine expectations of the friends of this laudable undertaking. The whole was concluded by an appropriate address on the part of the Lecturer, who, for the present, retired from his scientific labours amidst the well-earned plaudits of a numerous auditory.

'eligible apartments'

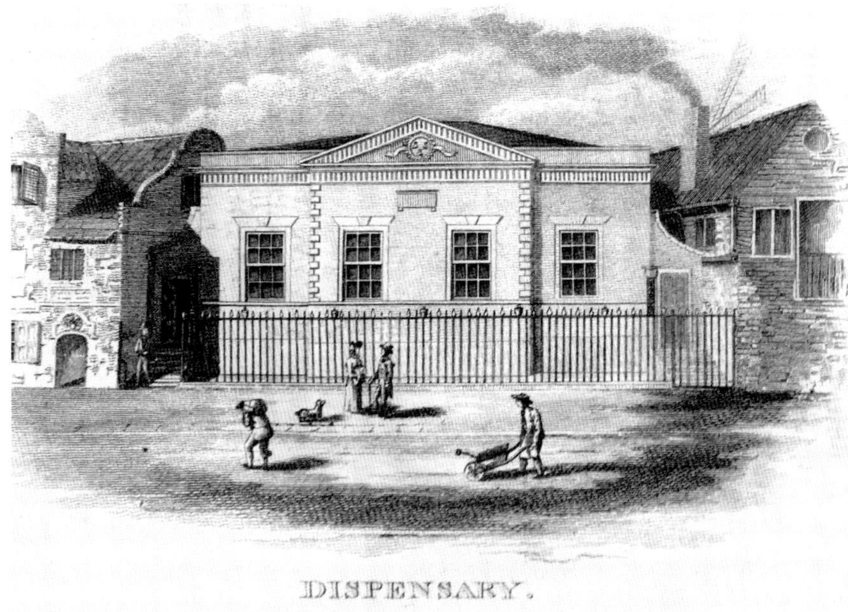

DISPENSARY.

This elegant building on Low Friar Street was built in 1777 as a Masonic Hall. But it wasn't long before "extravagance and the introduction of politics" caused the downfall of the Lodge, and the recently established Dispensary moved in. (The building was demolished in the 1930s, but Dispensary Lane still marks the spot.)

For the first year of its existence, the Society had rented a room in the Dispensary for its monthly meetings. But as the year progressed, there were books to accommodate as well as people. A local carpenter was commissioned to build an 18 foot bookcase which did the job handsomely - until it didn't.

They had to find new premises. Then rent two rooms. Then move again. Increasingly, the Society's accommodation requirements were complicated by the broadening of its role and the steady acquisition of physical paraphernalia.

Firstly, a collection of books hadn't originally been provided for, but the Society began to acquire books immediately and apace. Then there was the Society's rapidly growing "museum". The complement to a library, it contained specimens from rocks to plants, from insects to stuffed mammals, from classical Rome to contemporary Australia, all furthering the cause of philosophical enquiry. Thirdly, with the establishment of the Lectureship it became necessary to acquire "valuable scientific apparatus" which required safe storage.

From 1797 the Society had occupied the "old Assembly Rooms" in Ridley Court off the Groat Market. Of course the collections went on growing. When in 1813 the proprietor served them notice, the Committee resolved to build their own permanent home. In 1815 members agreed that over and above their annual subscription of one guinea, for a fixed four-year period they would pay an extra half guinea per annum into a Building Fund.

The search for a satisfactory site was on.

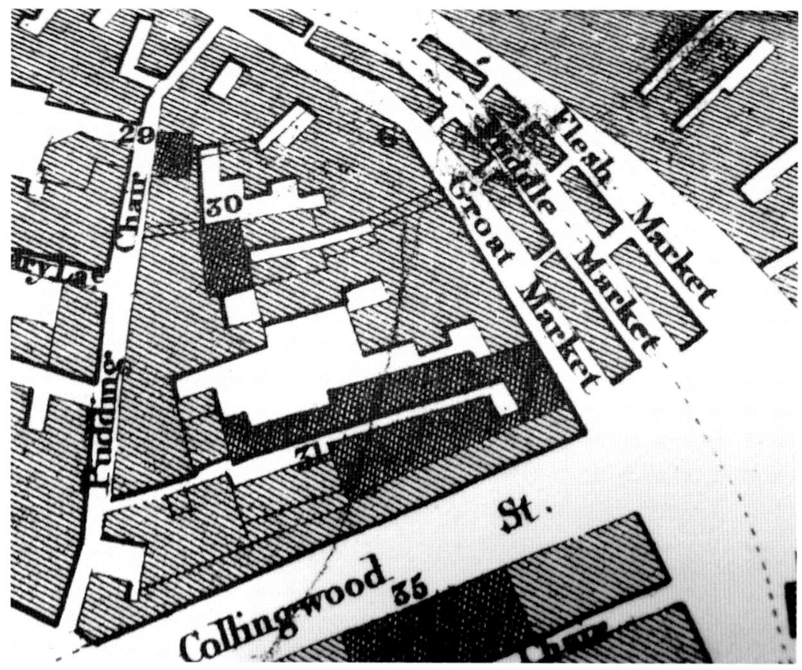

Ridley Court, Groat Market must have housed more than one interesting tenant. On Wood's 1827 map it's indicated by the letter G, one of only a handful of letters used in his key.

The ensuing years saw little useful progress. They were economically straitened years following the Napoleonic Wars. The Building Fund didn't get off to a flying start: ingenious schemes designed to entice the local aristocracy to dip into their pockets failed to elicit the desired response.

One local aristocrat who demurred rather volubly was Sir Charles Monck. Sir Charles was currently engaged in building himself the grandest of private homes, Belsay Hall. In 1815 he communicated his excuses to the Society. They expressed scruples which sat uncomfortably with his own huge project. His chief argument was the "moral harm" that would be done to young people of limited means, if the project intended for their benefit received donated funds rather than requiring their equal contribution. He also questioned why a learned society should lavish money on bricks and mortar at all. This is an early hint of the faction that was to become increasingly divisive among members.

Meanwhile half a dozen potential locations were considered, but "various objections" to each one were raised by various members of the committee. For the time being, the pressure to leave Ridley Court eased off. In 1817 the Society adapted the premises to suit their needs better, modernised them by the introduction of gas lighting, and remained in cramped occupation.

By 1821, intolerable pressure on the Ridley Court space made crunch time inevitable. But old Committee differences still proved intractable. Short on funds, they were long on diverging opinions on how funds should be spent . . .

It looked like impasse, until an act of old-fashioned philanthropy moved things on.

'liberal offer'

Without the intervention of twenty-six generous (and exasperated?) members, who knows how the Society's story would have unfolded. Their names are all recorded, but one name is remembered above the others. It was the respected Dr Headlam, himself a committee member, whose initiative brought the twenty-six together.

In November 1821 Dr Headlam made the Committee an offer. He and his friends would, "at their own risk", jointly purchase Mr Angas's freehold property on Westgate Street; and for £1,000 the Society could buy from them a plot of suitable dimensions to accommodate the building they required.

Further quibbles would be curmudgeonly. The building fund was still receiving members' half guinea contributions, thanks to a renewal of the four year term. By now it stood at around £2,200. A mortgage to finance the erection of a suitable building was a reasonable proposition. In perhaps grudging unanimity, the Committee accepted the offer.

'a more commodious receptacle for the increasing property of the establishment'

Paralysis was cured. Immediately after accepting Dr Headlam's offer, the Committee took advice on building requirements. In January advertisements appeared in newspapers in Newcastle, Durham and Edinburgh. They invited architects' plans, with estimates, for a building of specified parts with a specified budget of £3,600.

By February, no fewer than twelve sets of plans had been received. Some came from architects with established reputations, but these tended to exceed budget (some ridiculously so). The most modest estimate came from a thirty-four year old builder from Corbridge, lacking formal training and - as yet - a reputation as an architect. John Green.

In March a Building Committee of eminent members was elected to manage all aspects of the project, including choosing the winning design. But really, there was no choice. John Green's plans were the only ones which didn't exceed budget. In April his appointment was confirmed.

Contracts were finalised. The budget was raised to £4,000, to cover the purchase of re-usable materials from the "old houses" to be demolished on the site. Demolition went swiftly ahead. It was time to plan the ceremonial laying of the foundation stone.

John Green's pre-demolition sketch of the site showing the condemned "old houses".

'The Day Appointed'

The events of Monday September 2nd, 1822 were extensively reported in the local press. They have largely come down to us via the genial, if tongue-in-cheek, account supplied in Robert Spence Watson's history of the Society: Royalty arrives, the Town goes wild, masonic processions lead off, Royalty wields the trowel, the company removes to a sumptuous banquet at the Assembly Rooms, alcohol is liberally quaffed, toasts are interminably drunk, the "animated day" ends in boozy hilarity.

Spence Watson's irony serves to distract from aspects of the story which were too sensitive to expose. Probe deeper into the Hedley Papers, and a troubled narrative emerges. It's not too much to say that what members of the Society experienced that day, far from hilarity, was humiliation and outrage. This is an extract from the minutes of the first general meeting after the occasion:

"The Rev Mr Smith gave notice that at the next meeting the Society call upon the Committee to state what steps were taken by the Committee to preserve the dignity and respectability of the Literary and Phil. Society at the laying of the foundation stone of the new building."

Rev. Smith was persuaded to withdraw his challenge, but not before it had stung a smarting Rev. Hedley into responding. Loyal and long-suffering Secretary, Hedley attempted to pen a dignified catalogue of the frustrations that had been heaped upon the Committee throughout the summer. He filled six foolscap sides with his version of events before breaking off defeated. His truths would rock too many boats.

Still, he couldn't bring himself to tear up his testimony. He folded the densely covered sheets to fit inside his record book, and taped them back to back with Rev. Smith's notice. They appear to have been waiting two hundred years for their hearing.

A page from Hedley's statement, now almost too brittle to unfold.

'the usual ceremonies'

Without preamble Hedley takes up the thread which so rapidly became a disastrously knotted noose. Its source lay in the very person of the Society's aristocratic President, Sir John Swinburne Bar[t] of Capheaton. Fatally, among his other distinguished credentials Sir John held the office of Provincial Grand Master of Northumberland's Free Masons.

Sir John Swinburne, 1762-1860

No sooner did the region's numerous fraternity of Freemasons scent the opportunity than they "intimated" to the Committee that they desired the foundation stone to be laid with masonic honours. The Committee recognised that they could hardly insult their President by rejecting the masonic intervention. They wrote to Sir John, making it plain that his wishes would guide their decisions. When Sir John finally replied, his letter was a prevarication: he couldn't give them dates when he would be available and the occasion might have to go ahead without him.

From that point Sir John became vanishingly elusive, particularly after it emerged that HRH the Duke of Sussex, Grand Master of the United Grand Lodge of Ancient Free Masons of England, would be visiting the north later in the summer. From somewhere came the murmur that if invited, the Duke himself would be willing to lay the Lit & Phil's foundation stone. Again the Committee could only refer the situation to Sir John, emphasising to him the Society's preference for a simple ceremony with their own President performing the honours. Again Sir John prevaricated, saying he would try to discover the Duke's wishes. He never got back to them.

Obliged to continue with their preparations regardless, the Committee soldiered on, trying to second-guess their President's wishes in the teeth of a gathering masonic hi-jack. When it reached Committee ears that the Duke of Sussex had graciously accepted an invitation to lay their foundation stone, they had to assume that this was the result of Sir John's negotiations with the Duke. They were powerless to prevent the Masons from organising a massive regional turnout of masonic lodges; they couldn't object when the Masons wanted to construct a temporary amphitheatre on the Lit & Phil's site in order to accommodate their own great numbers; and they had to swallow the Masons' proposal to charge even Lit & Phil spectators for admission in order to defray the Masons' associated costs.

There was more to endure. The Masons wanted to round off the day's formalities in their own way, with a grand dinner. The Committee insisted on the Society's prerogative to decide on the matter. The Committee debated, and for reasons in line with their identity as a serious and unpretentious society, decided against a dinner. Before they had time to notify the Masons of their decision, they learned that the Masons were advertising an exclusively masonic banquet for the Duke.

The discourtesy was almost intolerable. But painfully the Committee agreed that the Society should preserve the appearance of calmness and decorum, as it would not "be at all advantageous to the character of the Society to betray a feverish anxiety for a participation in tavern revels."

The withering terms reveal the Committee's private opinion of masonic celebration. But as soon as the words had escaped his pen, Hedley must have known he could never speak them. That's where his manuscript ends.

Hedley's revelations put a fresh complexion on some of the memorabilia pasted into the record books.

There's the record of items buried with the foundation stone. The elaborate description of a showy local artefact doesn't suggest the hand of sober Philosophers.

THE FOUNDATION STONE OF THE
LITERARY AND PHILOSOPHICAL SOCIETY,
OF NEWCASTLE UPON TYNE;
LAID, SEPTEMBER 2. 1822.
BY
HIS ROYAL HIGHNESS AUGUSTUS FREDERICK;
DUKE OF SUSSEX.

THE following Coins were deposited in an elegant Glaſs Vase, 13 inches long and 3 inches diameter, richly cut with pointed Diamonds, strawberry Diamonds, Rings, and Twist; engraved with the Arms of his Royal Highneſs, and the following inscription, " Deposited by his Royal Highneſs Augustus Frederick, Duke of Suſsex; 2d. Sept. 1822." The stopper cut with pointed Diamonds, starred, and polished; and on the bottom was engraved, " Presented by Joseph Price, Proprietor of the Durham and British Sheet Glaſs Works, Gateshead; 1822. " The whole completed with a Cap, also richly cut to correspond with the opposite end.

GOLD.	A Sovereign
SILVER.	A Crown Piece
	Half Crown
	Shilling
	Sixpence
	Fourpenny Piece
	Threepenny Do
	Twopenny Do
	Penny Do
COPPER	A Farthing

all of the Reign of GEORGE. IV.

In the Vase was also deposited, a Report of the Society's proceedings in 1821 — and a List of the Members. And in a cavity in the stone was also placed a Brass plate, with an inscription commemorating when, and by whom, the stone was laid, and the Names of those gentlemen holding official situations in the society.

Newcastle, Privately Printed for John Sykes.

There's the design for the silver trowel commissioned for the royal fist. Its virtuosic engraving proclaims another proud local craft.

There are the tickets of admission to the ceremony of laying the stone, printed separately for Philosophers and Masons . . .

MEMBER'S ADMISSION TICKET
For laying the
FOUNDATION STONE
OF THE
LIBRARY, &c.
OF THE
LITERARY AND PHILOSOPHICAL SOCIETY,
Monday, 2nd September, 1822.

GRAND MASONIC CEREMONY
OF
Laying the Foundation Stone of the
LIBRARY, &c.
OF THE
LITERARY AND PHILOSOPHICAL SOCIETY,
Monday, 2nd September, 1822.
ADMISSION TICKET.

. . . and there's the single ticket, ostentatious with its red wax seal, for the masonic dinner. And then a twist. In one of the record books a humble hand-written card is pasted beneath the Masons' dinner ticket:

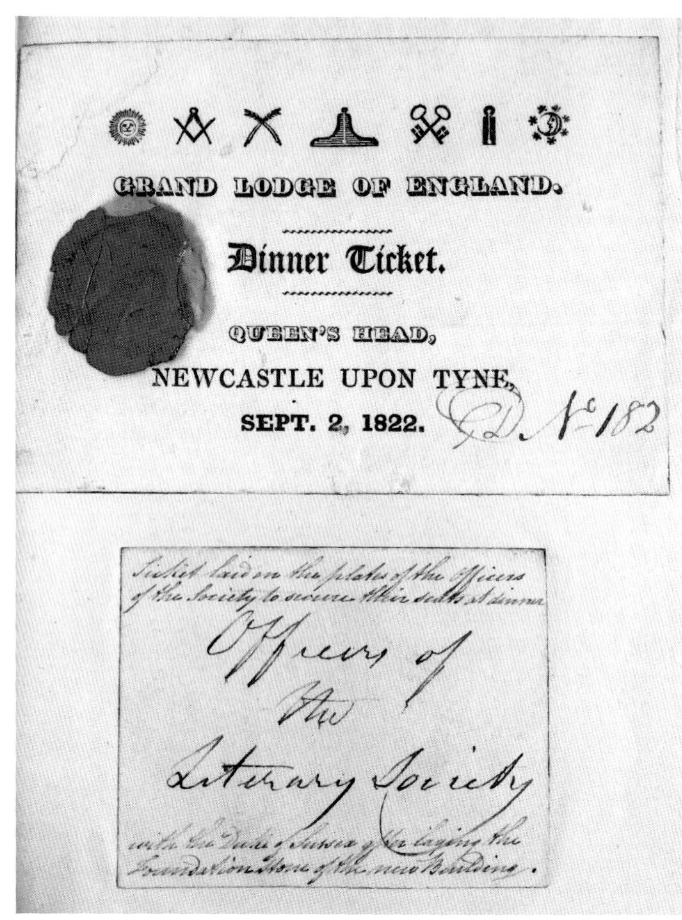
GRAND LODGE OF ENGLAND.
Dinner Ticket.
QUEEN'S HEAD,
NEWCASTLE UPON TYNE,
SEPT. 2, 1822.

Ticket laid on the plates of the officers of the Society to secure their seats at dinner
Officers of the Literary Society
with the Duke of Sussex after laying the Foundation Stone of the new Building.

It's hard to imagine a nib fine enough to produce the gossamer writing which reads "Ticket laid on the plates of the officers of the Society to secure their seats at dinner with the Duke of Sussex after laying the Foundation Stone of the new Building".

A handbill displayed in all the record books throws light on the eleventh-hour inclusion of Lit & Phil officers at the Masons' dinner. The Royal Voice had spoken!

LITERARY

AND

Philosophical Society.

THE DUKE OF SUSSEX

HAVING been pleased to signify his Wish, that the DINNER to be given to his Royal Highness on the Occasion of laying the Foundation-Stone of the New Library, on Monday next, should be a JOINT-DINNER of the Members of the Literary and Philosophical Society and the Free Masons, such Members as intend to do themselves the Honour of dining with his Royal Highness, are requested to give in their Names to Mr Dodsworth, of the Queen's Head Inn, as early as possible, but not later than 10 o'Clock on Monday Morning.

☞ Dinner in the Great Room of the Assembly Rooms, at Four o'Clock. Tickets, £1. 1s. each, to be had at the Bar of the Queen's Head.

31 Aug 1822.

S. Hodgson, Printer, Union-Street.

The date faintly seen in the bottom left hand corner is 31 Aug 1822. That was Saturday, with the great event imminent on Monday.

Even if Hedley had had the stomach to conclude his pained account, he'd have struggled for terms in which to tell the hardest bit. The ultimate, bitter humiliation was this: the Society's President didn't show up on the day. Unchampioned and hopelessly outnumbered, the Philosophers saw the integrity of their occasion swept away in a disorderly masonic spree.

Sir John had last been heard from in the middle of July, communicating on a matter of Society finance. He was about as far from the North East as it was possible to be, writing from an address on the Isle of Wight. A short closing paragraph refers to the foundation stone event. Its words aren't reassuring.

The less than exemplary handwriting reads: "I understand it is expected that the Duke of Sussex will lay the Foundation Stone of our new Building, if I possibly can reach the North in time, I shall certainly attend upon him, this must depend upon business, over which I have no control."

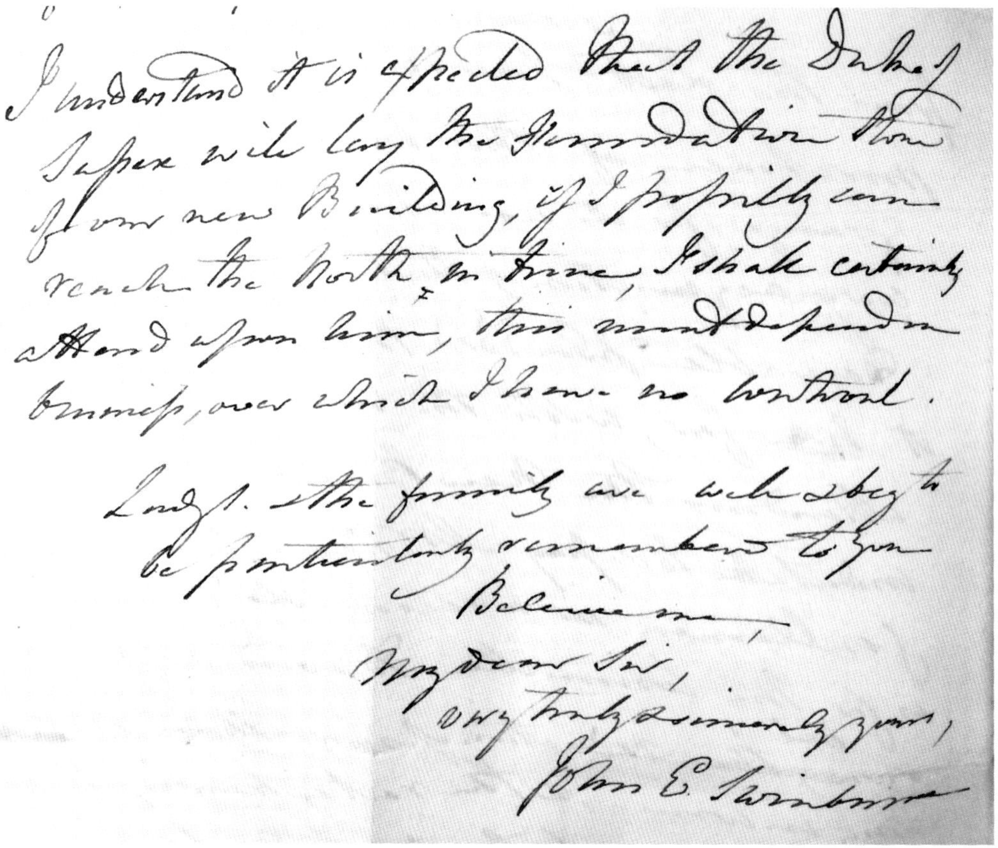
I understand it is expected that the Duke of Sussex will lay the Foundation Stone of our new Building, if I possibly can reach the North in time, I shall certainly attend upon him, this must depend on business, over which I have no control.

Lady S. & the family are well & beg to be particularly remembered to you

Believe me,

My dear Sir,

very truly & sincerely yours,

John E. Swinburne

The record books contain no further word of Sir John until September 3rd, the day after the great event. Suddenly, he's back in Capheaton, effusively regretting having missed the occasion. His letter offers three disingenuous excuses. First, mail not having reached him on his travels, he had "never had the most distant idea of the D of S's visit . . . till when I reached B Castle I found the Ceremony nearly over"; further, he had "been very unwell two days before"; and "besides, my protracted absence had accumulated business of great moment so that even a day's delay was of consequence".

The gentleman surely protested too much. The sorry fact was that the chemistry of Duke, Philosophers and Freemasons was too combustible for even a Baronet to handle. It's unlikely his excuses convinced his Committee, but you didn't question the word of your President.

And that's how it came about that the brass plate placed "in a cavity" in the foundation stone not only emphasises Masons above the Lit & Phil, but also bears an inscription which isn't entirely accurate.

THIS
FOUNDATION STONE OF A NEW BUILDING
To be erected for the use of the
LITERARY & PHILOSOPHICAL SOCIETY
of
NEWCASTLE UPON TYNE.
Was laid on the Second Day of September 1822 by
HIS ROY^{L} HIGH^{SS} PRINCE AUGUSTUS FREDERICK
DUKE of SUSSEX & EARL of INVERNESS in GREAT BRITAIN,
BARON of ARKLOW in IRELAND,
KNIGHT of the MOST HON^{BLE} ORDER of the GARTER,
PRESIDENT OF THE SOCIETY OF ARTS,
COLONEL OF THE ROYAL ARTILLERY COMPANY. &c.
And Most Worshipful Grand Master of the
UNITED GRAND LODGE
of
ANCIENT FREE MASONS OF ENGLAND.
Assisted by
SIR J.E.SWINBURNE BAR^{T} F.R.S & F.S.A.
PROVINCIAL GRAND MASTER OF NORTHUMBERLAND AND
PRESIDENT OF THE LITERARY & PHILOSOPHICAL SOCIETY.
And by
J.G.LAMBTON ESQ^{R} M.P.
PROVINCIAL GRAND MASTER OF DURHAM.

A footnote:
The Committee weren't so deferential as to spare their president some account of the fiasco. Sir John's ensuing correspondence shows him at such pains to be friends with his Committee that one might suspect a guilty conscience.

One year later, Sir John resigned his Provincial Grand Mastership. He remained the Lit & Phil's President for another sixteen years.

1822-1825

'A Building Calculated to Accommodate the Society'

Newcastle Courant, 12 January 1822

TO ARCHITECTS AND BUILDERS.

THE COMMITTEE of the LITERARY and PHILOSOPHICAL SOCIETY of NEWCASTLE will be glad to receive, on or before the 18th February next, PLANS (with Estimates) of a BUILDING to be erected for the Society's Accommodation. It is proposed that the Building should have a Stone Front, and a handsome Entrance and Stair-case; at the End fronting the Street; on the Basement-story, a Lecture Room, with Rooms for the Apparatus and Museum of Natural History, and also Apartments (not less than two), to be let to the Antiquarian Society; above, a Library, 80 Feet by 40 Inside, with a Gallery round. The Whole not to exceed £3600.

A Plan of the Ground may be seen at the Society's Library in the Groat Market.

N. B. The Author of the Plan approved of will receive twenty-five Guineas.

By Order of the Committee,
WILLIAM TURNER, } Secretaries.
ANTHONY HEDLEY, }

'a Stone Front . . .'

The Committee didn't spell it out, but they hardly needed to. We call the style Greek Revival. They called it Grecian. 1820s Britain loved it.

It had been coming since the previous century. It started as a romantic predilection for the architectural forms of antiquity, partly driven by the expanding leisure pursuit of tourism. In particular the country's élite youth was sent on the "Grand Tour" of European capitals, ostensibly to consolidate their élite classical education by studying the great art of ancient civilisations. Rome and Athens were top destinations. Books were published, images circulated.

For some it went beyond a fashionable hobby. In 1762 the British architects James Stuart and Nicholas Revett published the first volume of their immaculately illustrated, full folio work "Antiquities of Athens". It had an immediate and enduring influence on architecture throughout Britain and beyond. Four more volumes of their drawings were gradually published.

Assembly Rooms 1776

In civic architecture, neo-classicism first aimed for general effect. You didn't have to master the principles of Greek proportion to apply random classical features to a building. Newcastle's new Assembly Rooms on Fenkle Street opened in 1776, sporting a splendid neo-classical façade with an eclectic array of styles in the mix. It lent pomp to a venue specifically designed for "elegant recreation", but didn't pretend to antique authenticity.

Public taste became better informed and more particular. A preference began to emerge for the uncluttered sobriety of ancient Greek architecture. Not only for its satisfying aesthetic, but also because it was seen to have a moral dimension. In 1812 the new Moot Hall on Castle Garth wasn't created to serve fashion. Its stern Greek lines deliberately evoked associations of a society civilised by the authority of law.

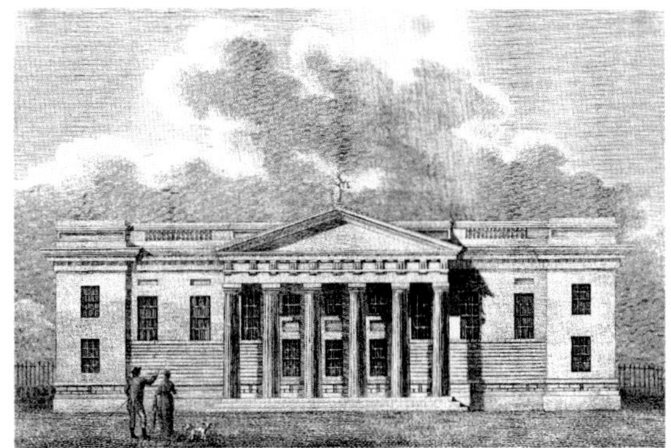

Moot Hall 1812

It went further. A classical education taught that Ancient Greece was the birthplace not only of democracy, but also of optimistic ideals of human potential and rational progress. If a building designed as a seat of learning looked like a Greek temple, that building was its own bright message.

John Green was no novice in the Grecian style, and the manuals were at hand. He had a temple to create.

Plans

The ground plans were relatively straightforward. The original remit had already specified the apportioning of space and the overall dimensions. We can't be sure that the two unsigned plans pasted into the Hedley Papers represent Green's original winning entry, but it seems likely that's why they're preserved there.

The plans deliver to the letter. Green wasn't to know that before they could be translated into hard masonry, a series of changes would be introduced. It transpired that the Building Committee were still deciding what they really wanted.

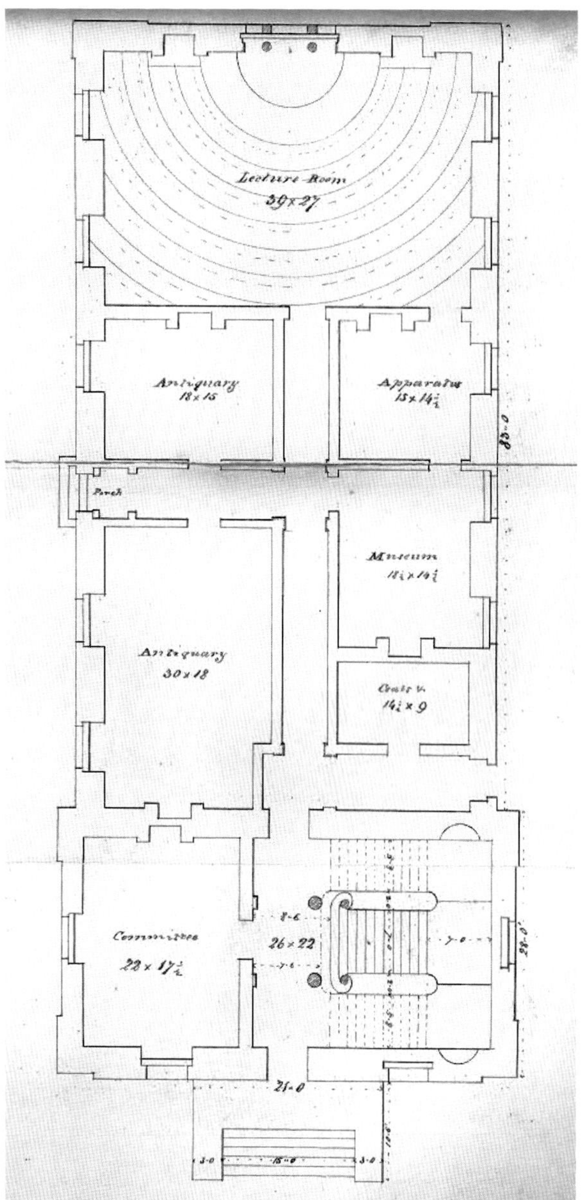

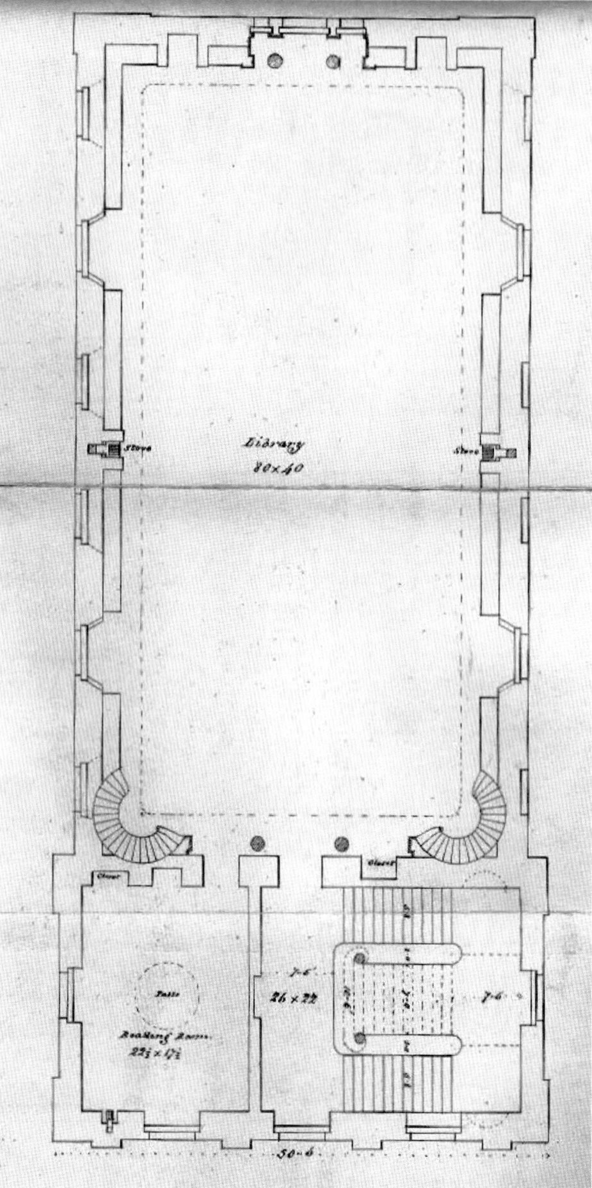

Shadow Plans

If the plans appear light on provision for utilities, it's because in 1822 there were virtually no utilities to provide for.

Heating was largely supplied by the traditional means of fireplaces. Green has indicated numerous fireplaces in his plans, but he didn't need to identify such essentials.

Lighting would need some planning now that gaslight was a requisite, but this wasn't in the architect's remit. The Building Committee expected to consider options themselves, at an appropriate stage of construction.

Water was a commodity to be accessed outside the building. In 1822 it was still a rare establishment that rejoiced in the privilege of an erratic piped water supply.

There are no formal records for such mundane domestic details. The relevant work was done on an ad hoc basis, beneath the radar of minuted meetings. If an item incurred undue expense, it was brought before the members, minuted and published in the annual reports. Otherwise there's silence.

But we're not left completely in the dark as to the Committee's intentions. The annual accounts itemise each purchase and each reimbursement made on the Building Committee's behalf. Expenses in respect of what the Building Committee classified as "fitting up" and "outdoor jobs" naturally occur towards or after the end of the main construction period. They bear on outcomes rather than plans, but for convenience, the outcomes are indicated here as extensions of the 1822 plans.

For instance, the accounts for the year ending March 1825 shed further light on the heating arrangements. Payments are recorded not only for grates and fenders, but also for "Hot Air Stoves" and "Hot Air Pipes". It looks as if the function of the two stoves marked on Green's first floor plan was more sophisticated than meets the eye.

Again, during the financial year ending March 1826, the sum of £3.5.2 was paid to Mr James Watson for "sinking a well". The following year Mr Ions the mason was reimbursed for a number of jobs extra to his contract, including "Flagging in Yard and building Coal House, Water Closet, Well . . ." A separate entry for "digging Drains and Tank" might or might not refer to plumbing for the Water Closet.

The detail from the 1859 Ordnance Survey map comes a few decades later than the original building and shows subsequent internal alterations, but in the top left hand corner three outhouse buildings are clearly marked. Today they are dilapidated almost beyond recognition, but one of them was the Society's first Water Closet.

One commodity gave rise to such eye-watering expense that in 1827 the members had to be informed. The culprit was the Society's gas supply. Over the years the accounts refer to Gas Pipes, a Gasometer, a Tank for the Gasometer, a "capacious gas house" created by "inclosing" and roofing over the yard, and slating for the roof of the gas house. The ultimate fate of this scheme belongs to a later stage of the story.

Elevations

In 1822, the architect's immediate challenge was the façade. It was Green's big opportunity. The Hedley Papers have preserved two early sketches.

In one sketch, four massive Doric columns support a grand portico whose features are faithfully Doric, the plainest of the Greek orders. The ground floor masonry is dressed in a "rusticated" style, using channelling between the blocks to create a rugged effect. The technique was a well-established neo-classical convention, although classical Greek temples had no use for it: where we need external walls, they had columns.

Behind his columns, Green's touch is less sure. Curves were not Greek, but a Roman innovation now going out of architectural fashion. The arches sit uncomfortably between the severe Greek lines. Above all, a portico on this scale must have been wishful thinking: the expense of those columns would have given the treasurer palpitations.

An alternative version shows the portico columns reduced to four pairs of pilasters. Spaced across the full width of the façade, they alter its proportions. The blank areas of masonry left above the first floor windows are relieved with a row of blind oblong windows.

Green hasn't relinquished all first thoughts. A diminutive pair of Doric columns remains, now squeezed inside a lingering, unfortunate arch.

It's still work in progress . . .

'the intended new Building'

Only a month after Green's appointment, by mid May a definitive design was ready for the engraver. After another month, with a little flourish, the Tyne Mercury newspaper offered for sale a limited edition of 100 proofs of the engraving previewing the Lit & Phil's intended New Library.

ENGRAVING
OF THE
NEW LIBRARY
OF THE
LITERARY & PHILOSOPHICAL SOCIETY
OF NEWCASTLE.
This Day is published,
At the Tyne Mercury Office,
AN ELEGANT PERSPECTIVE ENGRAVING of the NEW LIBRARY. Price for proofs on India paper, 9d. each. As the engraving is intended for the NEWCASTLE MAGAZINE, only 100 proofs are printed. 25 June 1822

Horizontal channelling has become the final choice for the stone front section. Green has elegantly solved the façade problem with single pilasters, spaced across a slight projection which faintly suggests the portico of the earliest sketch.

It was imposing. But it was never realised. If Green thought the job was done, he had reckoned without the Building Committee's emerging propensity to move the goalposts.

'many important alterations'

Within a month of the engraving's publication, the Society was contemplating a contentious acquisition. By August, the decision was taken: the entire "museum" of a deceased private collector was to be purchased. That made part of Green's plan obsolete, even before building had begun. The ground floor room originally designated for the Society's museum was now far too small. The only other space not spoken for was an equally unsuitable low-ceilinged attic room above the "reading room" and stairs.

Building commenced anyway in the autumn of 1822. Then an exceptionally severe winter delayed things. By the beginning of March 1823, the Building Committee had some ambitious new ideas to lay before the Anniversary Meeting.

One idea was already fait accompli. Stone had originally been specified only for the front section of the building. The other walls were to be done "in the common kind of walling technically called blocking course". But now there was talk of a future street which might run along one or other side of the building, exposing a full side to street view. The Building Committee explained that they had found themselves "dissatisfied with the appearance" of their intended side walls. The "rustic channelling" settled on for the front was already being continued all round the building. The Building Committee hoped that Members would sanction the extra expense of £161 which they had "in their discretion ventured to incur".

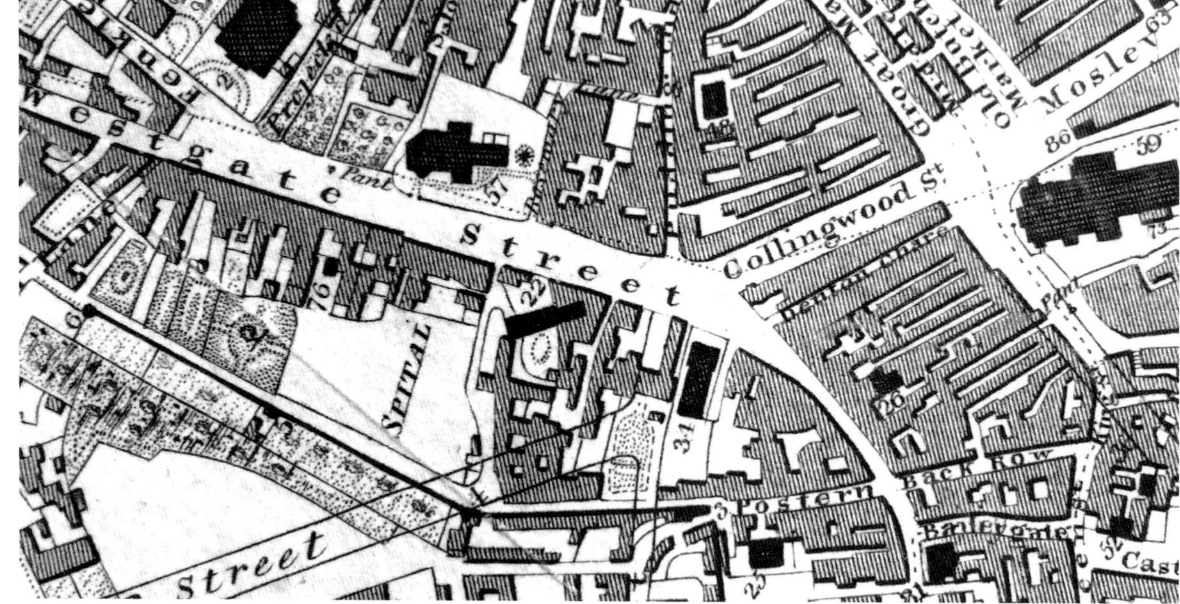

The Corporation's town development plans included a south-westward extension of Collingwood St. The precise route of the new street was still under discussion. Oliver's 1830 Plan "Shewing the Projected Improvements" illustrates one option which would spare the Grammar School from demolition by sacrificing Westmorland Place, to expose the Lit & Phil's west wall.

Another rethink was far more sweeping. Of course Green must have been involved in this. The Building Committee wanted to raise the planned height of the building by 4 feet. They argued to the meeting that a higher ceiling in the "great room", instead of a previously mooted central dome, would place the room's intended grandeur beyond doubt; also that an extra four feet would improve the façade's proportions; and that in the space gained above the stairs a suitable Museum room could be created across the whole front of the building.

The Building Committee estimated that the "whole expense of the building, as now erecting, will be somewhere about £5,000". They sought the meeting's consent to this further inflation of the budget, offering the appeasement that members might think their disappointment "to be more owing to the too sanguine expectations of the Society, than to the Committee's improvidence".

NEW LIBRARY.

You could be sceptical about the emphasis on appearance, but you couldn't deny the practical case for the Museum. The vote was carried, and the architect returned to his drawing board.

There's some artistic wizardry going on in this 1827 engraving of the end result. It's the computer-generated image of its day, manipulating perspective to emphasise the desired noble impression. Green's detail hasn't greatly changed, but now three loftily alert attic windows dignify the upper façade and finally, the entrance has been squared off. Doric integrity was realised - almost. If the purists wanted to niggle, they still had those little columns in the doorway.

And so the Philosophical Society's Library, liberated from offending arches and resplendent from every aspect, received its Stone Front. The budget, however, received a body-blow.

'a spacious vestibule'

The "handsome Entrance" is north-facing. Green's early plan includes a porch, with obvious virtues in a northern climate. The fashionable Assembly Rooms lacked this amenity, an absence lamented by patrons descending from their conveyances in evening finery. But the evolution of Green's façade put paid to porches. Visitors could at least be glad they were arriving in day clothes.

Continuity between outside and inside was part of the classical concept. Alas for Green's aesthetic sensibilities if he were to pass between his Doric columns today! Dimness and clutter are the antithesis of the first impression that he desired his interior to convey.

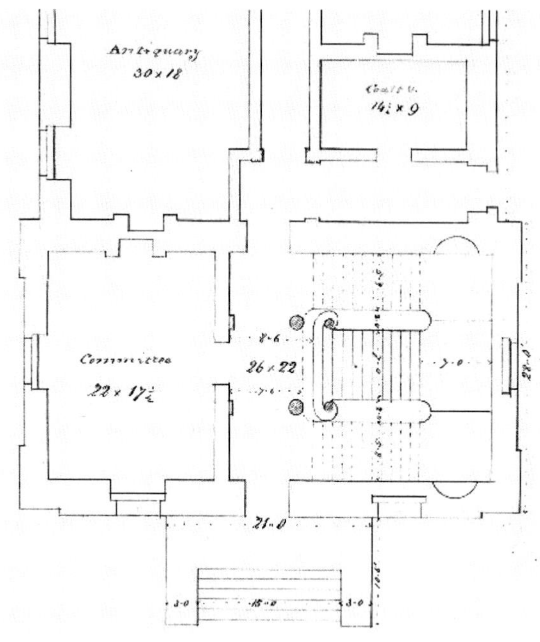

Seen from the street, a ground floor window appears to light the foyer. But the plan shows that window designed blind, obstructed by the upper flight of stairs. Daylight came from the first floor windows.

The elegant stairs were the stunning focal point, with their "exquisite" iron-work railings and sweep of gleaming brass handrail. Keeping this bright was one of the servant's catalogue of daily duties. The stairs rose towards a full length window on the first landing. The potential of a west-facing window was sadly compromised by the grimy presence of Westmorland Place immediately beyond its panes. You'd need a discreet blind.

Airy space is what Green's design evoked. The décor invited you to imagine a courtyard. Empty of portraits and sombre timber panelling, from flagged floor to coffered ceiling the walls were uniformly light, probably painted to echo the ashlar blocks outside. Simple expanses of wall and stone flag were the sole backdrop for the star feature, the "noble stone staircase". The staircase was "in appearance exceedingly light". Green had designed a hanging central flight to match the upper flights, the uninterrupted expanse of flags running from wall to wall beneath it, enhancing the spacious effect. (Could these flags be some of the materials retrieved from Mr Orde's house?)

The first landing was decorated only by two plaster casts of a famous antique "urn" excavated in the mid eighteenth century. The original plan, probably never executed, places them in curved niches at each end of the landing, tactfully allowing the stairs to monopolise the limelight.

Further classical allusion came into its own as you turned towards the top landing. In five compartments over the upper stairs, casts of five of Lord Elgin's recently removed Parthenon marbles eternally enact the conflict between civilised man and his inner barbarian. Sheltered Newcastle eyes were challenged. No one said mythology was modest.

Handsome entrance? The untried young architect was socking it to them.

'opening the Lecture-room'

The Anniversary Meeting of March 1824 optimistically reported to its members that the delayed building had now progressed so rapidly that the Society "may assure itself of the certainty of being in the occupation of it before the close of the year." Accordingly, the meeting's business included arrangements for the first ever series of lectures to be held in the Society's own lecture room.

The course of twenty-four lectures was to commence in the first week of October. Admission to the course would be free to members, one guinea to non-members, and half a guinea for ladies and under twenty-ones. Admission for a single lecture would be a pricey two shillings and sixpence.

The timing might have been touch and go. They didn't quite manage the first week of October. But on October 18th 1824, the lecture room welcomed its maiden audience, assembled to hear the Society's senior lecturer, the Rev. W. Turner, open his new season's series of lectures on Chemistry.

Since 1825, the ground floor beyond the stairs has undergone so many alterations that today hardly a trace remains of the original layout. Green's plan and a couple of underwhelmed comments are our only record of this first lecture room. It was designed in customary amphitheatre form, but the rudimentary compass arcs offer no information on seating arrangements, presumably benches.

The room is two side windows deep, making it the size of today's Loftus Room. It was said to accommodate an audience of up to 280. How did such numbers ever squeeze into their seats? Were the ends of the front two rows really in such roasting proximity to the fireplaces?

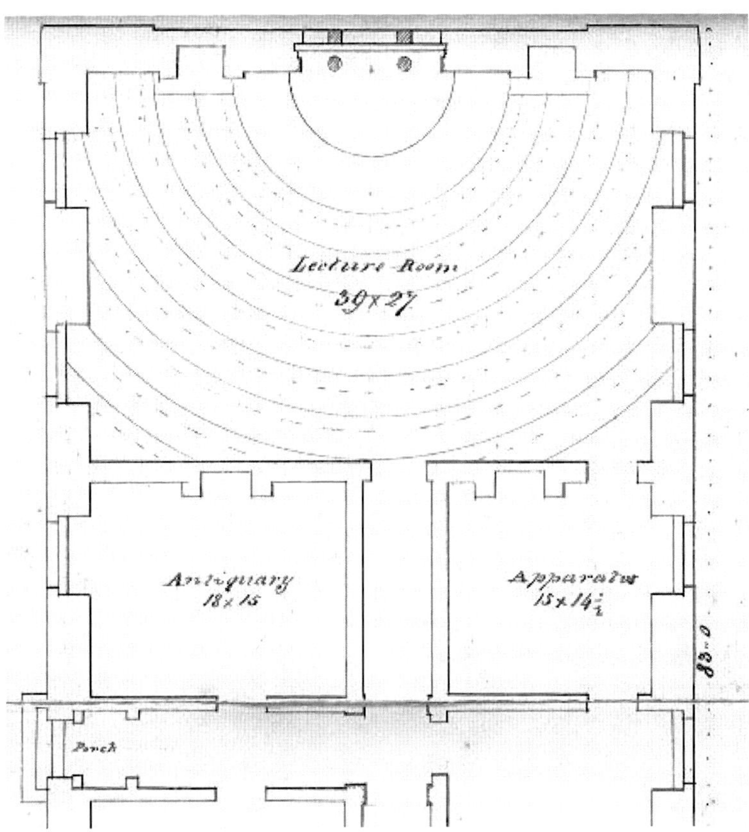

It's on record that the lecturer had to navigate a hazardous path through the press of people to get from the apparatus room to his table.

"Not a pleasant place" observes Robert Spence Watson.

'other deviations from the original plan'

The respectful feet of the first lecture audience didn't enter a completed building that autumn, nor was completion imminent.

By the time of the March 1825 Anniversary Meeting, mutterings must have been audible. The Building Committee recorded neither explanation nor apology. Their report strikes an upbeat, even self-congratulatory note. The work was now "so forward" that by the end of the month little or nothing would remain to be done, and - they implied - its superior quality couldn't have been achieved in a shorter time.

"The Committee trust that, without incurring the risk of too highly appreciating the result of their own labours, they may confidently appeal to [the building] as completely fulfilling all their former promises . . ."

The original criterion of economy had unapologetically given way to one of style:

"Almost every part of the Building has been finished in a better style than was at first intended, which has insensibly led to expense."

It wasn't only the finishing. A particularly expensive "deviation" from the original plan was ongoing this year. During 1824 the Building Committee had seen fit to spend £480 on the purchase of a further piece of ground behind the building. Now they had undertaken the repair of some old premises there to provide accommodation for "a servant". The considerable net outlay was justified to members on grounds of the rent that the said servant would pay the Society.

The business of the current year "related principally to points of minor detail". The minor details looked rather substantial when listed, entailing new contracts often for work as yet unpriced: a wall on ground behind the building, "malleable gates", cast iron railings to the street, a parapet wall for these, gallery railing, fireplaces, four marble chimney pieces.

Marble supplied the outward splendour of the fireplaces; their innards had been accounted for in March 1824, when the gratified Building Committee reported the condescension of the Society's patron His Grace the Duke of Northumberland in permitting them to source the stone required for "a part of the chimney pieces" from his private quarry at Denwick. Apparently noble obligation had its limits: the 1825 accounts show outgoings for the quarrying of 4 tons of stone at Denwick, its carriage to Alnmouth, and its transport by sea to Newcastle.

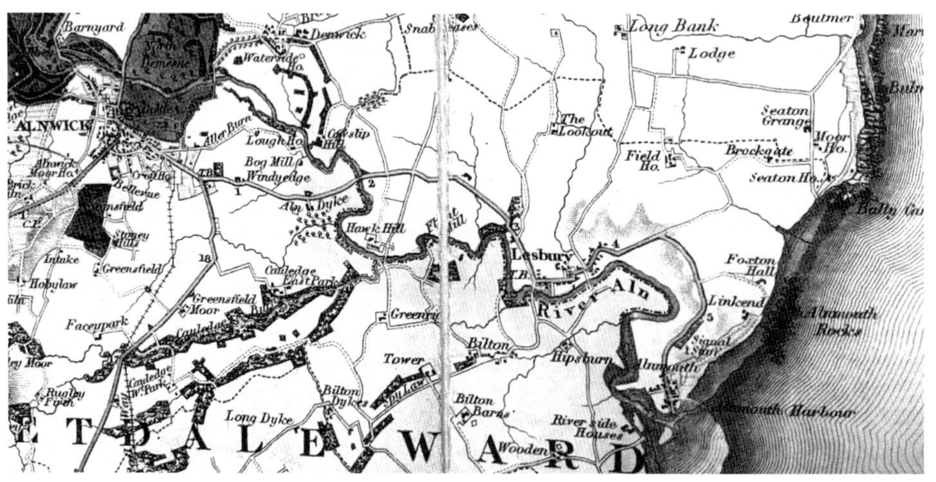

The detail from C.&J. Greenwood's 1828 Map of the County of Northumberland shows the first lap of the stone's journey, from Denwick in the north to Alnmouth Harbour.

None of this work was budgeted for. The Building Committee explicitly shunted the blame: the work now falling to their charge had "certainly not been taken into consideration by the [main] Committee" when calculating the original budget. They didn't mention that the main Committee also certainly hadn't taken into consideration the extravagance of its Building Committee's decisions.

Even in full recognition of the staggering overspend, there was no deflecting them from their single-minded pursuit of the grandiose. The list of contracts concludes with the information that the stone front steps have now been extended to reach across the full width of the front. The report describes this alteration as "a change which, there can be no doubt, though somewhat expensive, has materially added to the beauty and imposing appearance of the exterior".

Since the somewhat expensive steps were about to be enclosed by a parapet wall with railings, their aesthetic contribution might have been almost as questionable as their practical usefulness.

'the mode of lighting the Building'

The early century's innovation of gas lighting would be grist to a Philosophical Society's mill. But the technology was still evolving, and the moment had come when the Building Committee had to get to grips with practicalities.

They reported to the March 1825 meeting that having considered "every information they could obtain", they had determined that it would be more economical and efficient for the Society to produce its own oil gas, than to pay the Corporation for its coal gas (a "disheartening" 12s.6d per 1000 feet of gas). A small apparatus had duly been purchased for £51.11s ("exclusive of the gasometer"). The Building Committee trusted that members would approve. Construction of the requisite "gas house" to accommodate the apparatus is mentioned only in the 1826 annual report.

The newly opened library room was pictured in a water-colour by John Green's son Benjamin. The fashionable family group may be fanciful, but this detail beautifully records the building's various light fittings, as well as the windows at intervals round the gallery.

Servants were apparently cheaper than the Corporation's rates. In December 1825 the Society were looking for a married couple to employ as caretakers of the building. The manservant's "leading duty" was explicitly to maintain the gas supply in its many and various aspects. The Committee's detailed "Outlines of Duty of Two Servants" are printed in Appendix 2. They offer vivid glimpses not only of the processes of making and burning oil gas, but also of the daily running of the building.

In 1825 the Building Committee couldn't foresee that their decision to make oil gas would lead them down a fraught path of costly miscalculations. At the anniversary meeting of 1827 they were obliged to outline a painful two-year journey towards recognition that the Corporation's gas was the better option after all.

'wishful to open the Museum to strangers'

In July 1825 the building was finally reported "fit for the reception of the Society's library and other property". Immediately the library and museum were removed from Ridley Court into their new accommodation.

On November 21st the museum was opened between the hours of 12 and 3pm for the visits of members and friends of members. Another of the myriad duties required of the Society's toiling manservant was to "have himself cleaned" from his dirty morning chores, in readiness to attend the museum at midday. In March 1826 the anniversary meeting resolved that "strangers" might be admitted to the museum for one shilling, if accompanied by a member. The Committee regretted that the charge was unavoidable owing to the Society's financial embarrassments.

From street to attic was a long haul. No concessions to gammy knees: evidently lean, keen natural philosophers weren't expected to let a few stairs deter them from the privilege of viewing Newcastle's first and only museum. Besides, a number of rare specimens had gone missing from the Ridley Court premises. A supervisable stronghold was all to the good.

Placing a sprightly step on the final little staircase, the visitor would first set eyes on the fireplace in the wall directly opposite. It sat just where the central attic window is situated on the façade outside.

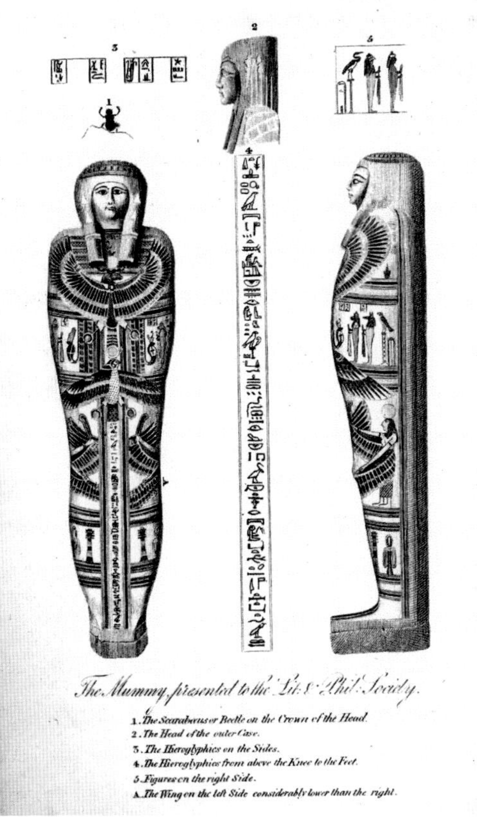

The Mummy, presented to the Lit: & Phil: Society.

1. The Scarabæus or Beetle on the Crown of the Head.
2. The Head of the outer Case.
3. The Hieroglyphics on the Sides.
4. The Hieroglyphics from above the Knee to the Feet.
5. Figures on the right Side.

A. The Wing on the left Side considerably lower than the right.

Since Green more or less extemporised the design of this room, it's not surprising that no plans survive. Perhaps the windows were initially intended to open to daylight. There's one which still does, at the west end of the room. But from the outset the room was "well lighted by skylights".

Wall space was too precious for windows. There were hundreds of specimens to display. The museum now included serious collections of plants, shells, insects, stuffed creatures of land, sea and air, minerals and rocks, antiquities, and some anthropological "curiosities". Notably the recently donated Egyptian mummy, which was said to have pulled in an estimated ten thousand visitors over eight days when exhibited in town!

Nowadays the purpose-built display compartments are disguised by inserted bookshelves. But the double rows of books betray the extra depth of compartments designed to display exhibits that don't line up neatly like books. The compartments struggled to accommodate them all. It wasn't Green's fault, but the room was "crowded to excess".

One solution is revealed in the detail from Benjamin Green's painting. Spot the mummy and a sister mummy who joined her in 1826!

help. The fusion of space, light and intricate detail offered an unequivocally breath-taking spectacle.

Collard's engraving was published in 1841, in a slim volume celebrating the "various splendid improvements" that by then had transformed central Newcastle. Collard's colleague Metcalf Ross wrote the accompanying text. Ross's descriptions of each feature of the library room are accompanied by a standard repertoire of rapturous epithets: 'noble', 'exquisite', 'elegant', 'tasteful', 'magnificent'. By the time Ross was writing, the coved ceiling had been "richly gilded", in accordance with Green's original but deferred plans.

Every visitor experienced the gasp:

"On first entering the large room, its ample dimensions, the noble chimney-pieces, the gallery with its tasteful and elegant railing, and the exquisite plaster-work that surmounts the whole, combine in giving it a grand and sumptuous appearance."

Benjamin's painting was subsequently lost to Newcastle - but not before William Collard had based his engraving on it. During 1823 Green had been granted indefinite loan of the Society's volumes of Stuart and Revett's "Antiquities of Athens". A sample page shown in Appendix 3 demonstrates their importance to him as he meticulously designed this interior. Farewell to plain Doric forms: a cornucopia of classical Greek motifs spills into every crevice of the plasterwork. Collard has permitted himself even more artistic licence with perspective than Benjamin's original, but the room didn't need their

That's not Ross, but the printer and publisher Eneas Mackenzie. He was on the Society's main committee and had witnessed the whole building project at first hand. He wrote it all up in a chapter of his major work on Newcastle, published in 1827.

It's that word 'first' that sounds the alarm . . .

'inferior to what might have been expected'

To put it mildly, Mackenzie has fault to find. He doesn't mince his words.

Poor overall planning of the "large room" has resulted in dangerous roof pressure, ill-judged placing of some of the plasterwork which exposes it to potential damage, and a window arrangement which creates distracting shadows. Furthermore, the two staircases to the gallery are "narrow and awkward". (Ladies with their ever-widening skirts would have been particularly inconvenienced.)

The rather charming curved staircases of Green's early plan never materialised. Pasted into the Hedley Papers is a crumbling pencil sketch apparently revising this design. Of the two corner staircases which replaced them, only one remains today. The now dismantled staircase in the left hand corner has left a curved trace of plaster which can still be seen, hidden in an alcove outside what was the reading room.

Mackenzie's criticisms didn't stop at the "large room". The lecture room is "very badly planned", the museum is "insufficient", the Doric columns in the entrance doorway "have no business there", the Elgin casts are "not the most happily chosen ornaments for a library", and the whole building is in the wrong part of town.

"On the whole, this building is certainly inferior to what might have been expected, considering the vast expense of its erection and interior decorations."

Thumbs down from one committee member then.

The outspoken Mackenzie was hardly impartial. He was an ally of the reputable architect John Dobson, whose own proposal for the building had been side-lined in favour of Green's. Dobson was the same age as Green, but he represented a new species of professionally trained architects. With some justification he saw himself as an authority on "Grecian" architecture. The source of Mackenzie's criticisms isn't far to seek.

John Dobson

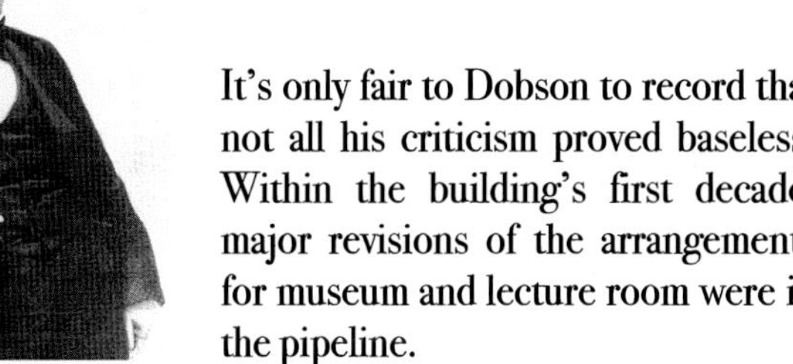

It's only fair to Dobson to record that not all his criticism proved baseless. Within the building's first decade, major revisions of the arrangements for museum and lecture room were in the pipeline.

'merely a fashionable lounging place'

Mackenzie had a second bone to pick. He was a political liberal, today's socialist. What mattered to him was not the building, but its contents and their egalitarian accessibility. He had been grieved by the unwarranted extravagance of such a building in the first place, never mind the sky-rocketing costs. The exorbitant outlay stuck in his craw.

He was at pains to praise where praise was due:

"it is proper to remark, that the workmanship is of the most superior description. Mr. Nicholson has executed the plaster-work with neatness and delicacy; the iron railings by Mr. Elliott shew great taste and skill; and the brass geometrical hand-rail by Mr. Watson is a fine specimen of accurate workmanship . . ."

But he knew where the extravagance would hit hardest.

The original member subscription had been one guinea per annum - perhaps negligible for the well-heeled, but a consideration for the "industrious classes". The additional half guinea payment into the Building Fund which members had agreed to in 1815 had never been discontinued, and in 1823 the Anniversary Meeting had been obliged to vote it a permanent increase. The accounts of 1827 brought on a further rise of the subscription to two guineas per annum.

Mackenzie's inexorable arithmetic demonstrated that even this imposition couldn't address the Society's debts. It would merely strike at its humbler members. He angrily spelt out where he saw it all going:

" . . . the annual payments would have to be again increased, and consequently the library would lose its former usefulness, and become merely a fashionable lounging place for the opulent classes of society."

The now 49 year old Mackenzie wasn't just being a grumpy old man. Appendix 4 tells the sequel to his predictions.

'*Paid to tradesmen . . .*'

At the 1826 anniversary meeting, the Building Committee "were unable to ascertain, with any degree of precision, the cost of the building, from a strange backwardness in the tradesmen employed to present their accounts."

Mackenzie again. The sarcasm wasn't a swipe at the tradesmen.

For Mackenzie and his friends, the Building Committee's house-keeping had been reckless to arrogant. Apparently no one on the distinguished Committee was competent, or willing, to make realistic calculations of the additional costs entailed by their changes of plan.

Contracts with the tradesmen had been agreed in the summer of 1822, before commencement of building. In March 1823 came the announcement that the revised plans would cost "somewhere about £5,000", and members had duly passed a resolution allowing the committee to spend an extra £1000. Since then there had been no apparent commitment to a budget. With a nod to the rising debt, the 1825 annual report reassuringly anticipated that an increased mortgage would ease the treasurer's difficulties. This proved over-optimistic: even in 1827, many of the tradesmen's accounts remained unpaid.

Repeatedly the Building Committee had justified its extravagance by reference to appearance. There was a sub-text.

Officially, it was rarely stated. Either they thought it went without saying, or they knew that saying it went against the progressive ethos that the Society was supposed to uphold. The fact was that a more conservative rationale was dictating the Building Committee's pretentious choices. Bred into their eighteenth century bones was the understanding that the cogs of social enterprise were oiled by patronage. Woo the aristocracy, and the aristocracy will be disposed to lend its invaluable support. Unfortunately the landed gentry weren't reliably susceptible to intellectual seduction. Grand interiors and posh steps were the way to go.

If the Building Committee was inclined to be coy about its accounts, Mackenzie wasn't. In his description of events he published a detailed breakdown of costs, many still unmet. Poor Mr Ions the mason became the late Mr Ions before the Society had fully settled their considerable account to him. In 1827 Mr Burnup the carpenter was still owed £600 and Mr Watson the gas fitter £550, to name only the most outstanding of the unpaid accounts.

"Somewhere about £5,000" had become somewhere over £13,000. Faces should have been as red as the Society's bank statement.

	PAID TO TRADESMEN. £.	s.	d.	TO PAY. £.	s.	d.
Ions (mason-work) -	3361	0	0	200	0	0
Burnup (carpenter) -	1458	10	11	600	0	0
Nicholson (plasterer)	904	4	0	...		
Archbold (slater) -	153	0	9	68	12	10
Marshall (plumber) -	267	14	10	...		
Elliott (smith) -	100	0	0	300	0	0
Watson (brass & gas works)	50	0	0	550	0	0
Cookson & Co. (iron-work)	...			172	10	0
Cooksons (plate glass)	100	0	0	154	17	8

	PAID TO TRADESMEN. £.	s.	d.	TO PAY. £.	s.	d.
Gibson (painter) -	160	0	0	200	0	0
Various (tables, &c.)	...			160	0	0
Green (chimney-pieces)	...			98	0	0
Jopling (ditto) -	21	6	10	...		
Bulman (hardware) -	...			174	15	9
Taylor & Co. (gas apparatus)	...			51	11	0
Green (architect) -	176	5	0	280	0	0
	6752	2	4	3010	7	3

	£.	s.	d.
Total paid - - - -	9048	7	$4\frac{3}{4}$
—— unpaid - - - -	3010	7	3
Interest due on the 7th March, 1826	156	0	0
Ditto to Mr. Fox ditto - -	39	7	6
Finishing yard, and building a very plain arcade say - -	400	0	0
Purchase of Museum by Mr. Fox	500	0	0
	£13154	2	$1\frac{3}{4}$

Mr. Angus' bill for the Museum is not included in the above account. The sum stated to be due to the architect is a mere guess, the precise terms of his engagement not being known. The other balances due, from the best information that could be obtained, are put down below their actual amount. The flagging and finishing of the yard, and the building of an arcade against the east wall, in which certain Roman antiquities are to be placed, cannot be done in a style corresponding with the principal building for the sum stated.---Richardson's executors have been paid off by borrowing the *L.*1500 of Miss Airey, at 4 per cent.

Mackenzie makes no bones about pointing the finger: ". . . the architect is not to be blamed, as he acted under the varying directions of a committee." Varying directions! There we have it. A shambles.

'a worthy shrine has been erected'

Nevertheless, there Green's building now augustly and irreversibly stood. It's to be hoped that the majority of those who crossed its threshold were animated by pride and excitement rather than chagrin and disgruntlement.

William Collard's book displays an engraving of the library's exterior after a drawing by "J. Green. Archt.". There's no mistaking the architect's message. Radiant in the sooty street, the sunlit façade bestows the benign light of learning upon Newcastle's fashionable citizens!

"This building stands in a conspicuous situation nearly opposite the west end of Collingwood Street" announces Metcalf Ross's text. Was that a clunky bid to harness a controversial project to the new street's shiny lustre? Ross, a Durham man, tiptoed gallantly round controversy: "Of [Green's designs] it is unnecessary to say more than that, by the taste, judgement, and skill of that gentleman a worthy shrine has been erected in which to deposit the works of the ancient sage and the modern genius."

For John Green there were no adverse repercussions. His work for the "Philosophical Society's Library" made his reputation. Publicly his building was praised as a noble achievement and a credit to the town.

Two hundred years on, the irony is that we can be only grateful for the Building Committee's excesses. Not only has the building endured, but it has endured as one of Newcastle's architectural gems. Moreover, it has remained in the hands of the Society which commissioned it, and by dint of ongoing adaptation has never ceased to fulfil the roles which the Society has required of it - while never ceasing to test the stamina and ingenuity of generations of committees.

For of course, Green's achievement marked not so much an end as a beginning. With barely a pause for breath, a new chapter of building and alteration was about to commence. And as the century progressed, unimaginable developments would present more than one new set of challenges.

That sequel is another story.

". . . the Nobility and Gentry of both the adjoining counties, who have proposed their names to be enrolled among us, express their satisfaction in having a place of occasional resort on their visits to this town, are pleased to introduce their friends to it, and have evinced a laudable emulation to promote . . its important objects . . ."

Anniversary meeting, March 1827

Appendix 1

Bourne and the Westmorland debate

The debate around the location of the original Neville site still intermittently raises its head. It seems to derive from different interpretations of Henry Bourne's words. It's not hard to see how it happens, as Bourne was himself searching for clarification. Bourne's presentation of the problem, and his inconclusive conclusion, are set out in two rather rambling paragraphs:

Sect. V.

Earl *of* Westmoreland's *House*.

NEXT to St. *Mary*'s, on the same Side of this Street, is a very old Building, which was lately the Dwelling-house of Sir *Robert Shaftoe*, Kt. *Recorder of this Town*, now the Property and Dwelling-house of Mr. *Charles Clark*, Junr. It has the Magnificence and Grandure of Antiquity in it's Looks; but what it has been formerly I could never find out. *Grey* tells us, That in this Street the Earl of *Westmoreland* had his House, which indeed is true. It was built by the Baron of *Bywell* and *Bolbeck*, about the 9th of *Edward* the Third. Much about the same Time he built a House within the Bounds of the *Castle*, for the Defence of it, as may be seen in our Account of the *Castle*. This House in *Westgate* was called *Bolbeck-Hall*; but afterwards, upon it's Founder's being created *Earl*, which was in the Reign of *Richard* the Second, in the Year 1398, when *Ralph Nevil*, Lord of *Raby* was created *Earl Marshall*, it got the Name of *Westmoreland-Place* in *Westgate*. Some have conjectured, that Sir *Robert Shafto*'s House, above-mentioned, was part of it; and indeed it looks much liker a Part of such a Building, than any other Thing remaining thereabouts. I am sure much more so than the House which is supposed to have been it, which I am told was the House opposite to the West End of *Denton-Chair*, which the Rev. Mr. *Cowling* lately lived in, and which belongs to Mr. *Ord*.

HOWEVER, be this as it will, whether it was this House now mentioned, or whether *Westmoreland-Place* reached from this House to Sir *Robert Shafto*'s, including it, which some have conjectured; yet this is certain, that it must have been hereabouts: For *Nevil Tower* is directly behind this Piece of Ground we are speaking of, which is a sure Token this must be the very Place; because, whoever in the Town built a Tower at their own Expence, it was generally nigh them for their own Security. Thus the *White-Fryers*; the Brethren of St. *Mary*'s Hospital; the Brethren of St. *Austin*, &c. Built their Towers over against their *Monasteries*, for their own Safe-guard and Security. But what I think puts it out of Dispute, that Sir *Robert Shafto*'s House was no Part of it, is that in the Eleventh of Queen *Elizabeth*, upon the Attainder of *Charles*, Earl of *Westmoreland*, this House where Mr. *Cowling* lived, was in Charge, which the other never was, before the Auditors; and in the Third of *Charles* the First, was sold to the Citizens of *London*.

IT was afterwards in the Tenure of *James Bertram*, and after that in the Tenure of *Robert Bertram*. [f]

In a nutshell, Bourne knows that in "about the 9th of Edward III" (i.e. about 1336), the "Baron of Bywell and Bolbeck" built a house "hereabouts". Quite whereabouts, four hundred years on no one can say. Bourne discusses the merits of current arguments, but in the absence of evidence he can't offer a solution.

His conundrum is that a "very old Building", bearing the appropriate Westmorland name, does exist, but it's standing in what ought to be the wrong place. Whereas in what ought to be the right place, a house stands that's plainly not old enough and doesn't carry the name.

The house in the right place, but looking too modern to qualify, was Mr Ord's. The house in the wrong place, which is "much liker" what Bourne is looking for than anything else in the vicinity, was "lately the Dwelling-house of Sir Robert Shaftoe, Recorder of this town".

Bourne's Preface plunges into a bitter background to his difficulties.

THE

PREFACE.

I Am ſenſible that this Performance will come into the World much more imperfect than I at firſt thought it would. But I have labour'd under ſo many Difficulties in the compiling of it, that when but a few of them are mentioned, I hope for a candid and favourable Judgment.

AFTER I had collected in private what Materials I could, I was then obliged to go publickly in Queſt of more. Upon this I publiſh'd an *Advertiſement*, deſiring the Aſſiſtance of ſuch as had ancient Writings, or Deeds, or any other Things that might contribute to the helping of the Work.

THIS immediately, occaſioned the following Reflections, that it might be of dangerous Conſequence to ſhew ancient Writings, that He was but a Curate that undertook the Work, that his Abilities therefore of Pocket and Mind muſt be vaſtly unequal to ſuch a Task; in ſhort, above 12 Months before the Publication of it, ſome have made it their Buſineſs, (ſo great has been their Ill-nature and Prejudice) as to take all Ways and Methods of decrying it; by Print, by Manuſcript, leſſening it in all Companies to hinder it's Publication, and ſpeaking as freely of of it, as if they were acquainted with every Line of it's Compoſition, and by a Prophetick Spirit knew it to be as they talk'd of it.

BY theſe Means I am certain I have been hindred of many Materials.

"Hindred of many Materials"! Poor Bourne. Ill-nature and Prejudice towards the scholarly Reverend had deliberately thwarted his best efforts. Because he was "but a Curate", the great and good didn't deign to cooperate with his requests. And detractors put out humiliating publicity to boot. Who needs social media.

The preface continues with particulars of "two grand Disappointments" that Bourne had met with, one directly relating to the Westmorland enigma. Hearing of the "large Collections of Sir Robert Shaftoe", Bourne explains, "I endeavoured after a Sight of them, but they were then either lost, or so mislaid, that there was no coming at them".

The Shaftos were local aristocracy, with a long history of high office in local and regional government. Shaftos had owned the so-called "Westmorland Place" since 1642. If answers were to be found anywhere, Sir Robert's Collections would surely be the place. Sir Robert had died in 1705, so Bourne presumably approached his heir. That was Robert's grandson, John Shafto of Whitworth, County Durham. John never occupied the house, and in 1731 finally sold it to its tenant Mr Charles Clarke. (For anybody wondering, the famous "Bobby Shafto" was John's first son, still the proverbial twinkle in his parents' eyes.)

The change of ownership would have been ongoing just around the time when Bourne was trying to track down his material. It was cruelly unfortunate timing. Whether John did or didn't try to oblige, this looks like the moment responsible for the ensuing centuries of confusion. A "grand Disappointment" for Bourne, and a can of worms for posterity.

Appendix 2

Servants required

In December 1825 the Committee drew up a detailed description of the duties of the "two servants" (a married couple) whom they required to look after the daily upkeep of the building. To twenty-first century eyes it looks like a superhuman workload, not to say inhuman exploitation. Maybe it was good fair employment for 1825, coming as it did with a "house of three rooms and coals".

There's some instructive detail on producing and using the house gas, on maintaining fires and fireplaces, on how to polish and dust what needed polishing and dusting, on the servicing of the hand-wash basin and outdoor water closet, on changes of dress to suit respective activities, on frequency of floor and step washing indoors and out, on keeping the entrance respectably clear of nuisance, including children and other loiterers.

Prior to the move into the new building, the Society's accounts show regular payment to "Mrs Affleck" for cleaning the rented rooms (final payment in the 1826 accounts amounts to £2.12.6). From 1827, Mrs Affleck's name disappears from the accounts, to be replaced by the untitled "Murton" who receives the sum of £65.0.0 for thirteen months' "attendance and cleaning the rooms". There's no mention of a Mrs Murton, but of course there wouldn't be. A wife was the property of her husband: she had no earnings.

OUTLINES OF DUTY

OF

TWO SERVANTS,

WANTED BY THE

LITERARY AND PHILOSOPHICAL SOCIETY

OF

NEWCASTLE UPON TYNE

THE MAN'S DUTY.

The leading part of his duty will be to make the gas, and to attend to the burning of it. As it is more economical to continue making it for some time, when once begun, as much must be made at once as the gasometer will hold. This will serve about three days, so that two days a week will be occupied with making it. As the operation is very simple, the whole time will not be requisite for it, only frequent attendance to to keep the fire up to an equal low red heat, and to see that the condensers are kept properly filled with oil. He must be careful to keep the apparatus very clean, and the gas-house orderly, otherwise it will be apt to get offensive.

As soon as evening sets in, he must light a few of the gas burners so as to make a moderate light through the rooms, & c. At seven, he must go round, and light all up fully, giving each burner a flame of 1 1/2 inch high, not more. This full light must continue till half-past nine, when the chandelier and all the burners not in use by the members must be turned down, and the whole light generally be reduced to one-half, or as little as may be found necessary. It will of course be his interest to be as careful of the gas as possible.

He must also keep the glasses, burners and pillars, clean and in proper order.

In his charge the fires will also be placed, as also the hot-air stoves. He must keep the fires up through the day, stirring and putting coals on when necessary. He must also be careful that the grates, and stoves, and hearths, &c. are kept well black-leaded; the fire irons and fenders clean, &c. He will be responsible for their being kept in proper order. The lighting of the fires in the morning, may be arranged between himself and wife.

He must also look after the front steps, and flags, and keep them clean, scrubbing with a broom and water, every morning, that part in front of the door. The whole should be scrubbed down once a week, but if advantage were taken of every heavy shower of rain, great labour on this point would be avoided. He must also look to the mats and scrapers, clean them every morning, and see them properly placed. He might also keep the flags at the foot of the stairs clean, but this his wife and he can arrange between them, but they must be cleaned every day. The outside rails, &c. he must also keep clear of nuisance; and the back yard and garden clean and orderly.

He will be expected to keep the urns, &c. in staircase, clear of dust.

When not making gas he will be expected to be constantly about the building, or at hand; to keep the entrance clear of children, and persons having no business there.

At twelve o'clock he must have himself cleaned, and attend the Museum, or as he may be wanted, from that hour to three. On the gas-making days, he might occasionally slip over, or get his wife to look to the fire.

At night he must assist the Librarian in locking up, and see that all the fires are put out, and the main gas cock turned off.

He must also see that the windows are kept clean.

As he will have much moving about amongst the Members, he will be expected to keep himself clean and orderly. His working dress, and which he might wear in the morning, may be a fustian or other jacket and trowsers, but these should be often washed. After 12 o'clock, his dress must be better, and for this purpose the Society will find a coat, waistcoat, and trowsers, every year. He should have some old clothes for the gas-house.

He must also take care that the water cistern above the water closet is kept filled, and that it is let off once a week.

The brass handrails of gallery and staircase he must also keep in order. If clean rubbed every morning with a clean cloth, or piece of wash leather, they will want little more.

Also the oak doors; these should be rubbed down, with a soft cloth, every morning or so, and the dust brushed out of the crevices; the handles and finger-plates kept bright.

Besides what is stated, he must endeavour to make himself as useful as he can, and to make it his study to keep the building and rooms in proper order, and as clean as possible.

He must also be ready to give his assistance whenever required. During the Lectures, his attendance or services will often also be wanted for them.

THE WOMAN'S DUTY

To her will be entrusted the cleaning of the building, and she will be considered answerable for its being kept as clean as a private house. To this end it seems necessary that the great room should be washed out every week, or at least every fortnight; and dusted with plenty of wet sand or saw-dust every morning; but the seldomer it is dusted and the oftener washed the better. The dirty parts about the door and tables should be washed every morning, or, as often as wanted. The stairs to gallery and museum should be cleaned same as room. The gallery may be washed only once a fortnight, and dusted when wanted. The gallery railing should be dusted as often as necessary.

All the empty shelves must be dusted once a month.

The museum must be washed out once a week, at least, and dusted every day.

The reading room must be washed out once a week; the dirty parts washed and the whole dusted every morning.

The staircase must be washed out once a week, in dirty weather twice; the dirty steps should be cleaned every morning.

The Committee room must be washed once a month, and dusted once a week.

The Lecture room the same; but in Lecture time it must be washed every Friday, and dusted every Tuesday.

The apparatus rooms should be dusted once a week, and washed when wanted.

The water closet must be cleaned regularly every morning.

The passage and side entrance must also be kept clean, by washing once a week.

The tables, chairs, &c, in great room and reading room, must be dusted every morning.

Water will have to be carried every morning to the wash-hand stand, and the dirty water brought away.

She should also scower the front steps occasionally for her husband.

The windows must be cleaned by her husband and her. The windows of the reading-room, staircase, and large window in great room must be cleaned once a week; once a month may do for the others, but they must be kept decent.

As she will be required to devote at least six hours a day to the building, it is considered that she will be able to get through great part of what is here mentioned, but when the great room &c. is to be washed, say once a week, she will be allowed an assistant.

The great room and reading room must be done the first thing in the morning; then the staircase; the other rooms, passages, &c. in the latter part of the day, and the museum, if it cannot be done in the morning, may be done after 3 o'clock.

Finally, the building must be kept perfectly clean, and for this the man and his wife will be considered answerable.

As great trust will be reposed in them, they will be required to produce unexceptionable characters, not only for attention and ability, but also for honesty and sobriety.

They will be required to live on the premises, and will be provided with a house of 3 rooms and coals.

Appendix 3

"Antiquities of Athens"

Stuart and Revett's five stunning folio volumes surveying ancient Greek architecture were published over a period of seventy years, until long after the deaths of both. Volume Five appeared only in 1830. In 1823 the Committee granted John Green indefinite loan of the volumes their library possessed.

A single page hardly begins to do them justice. But this page from the second volume leaves no doubt as to the use Green had for them.

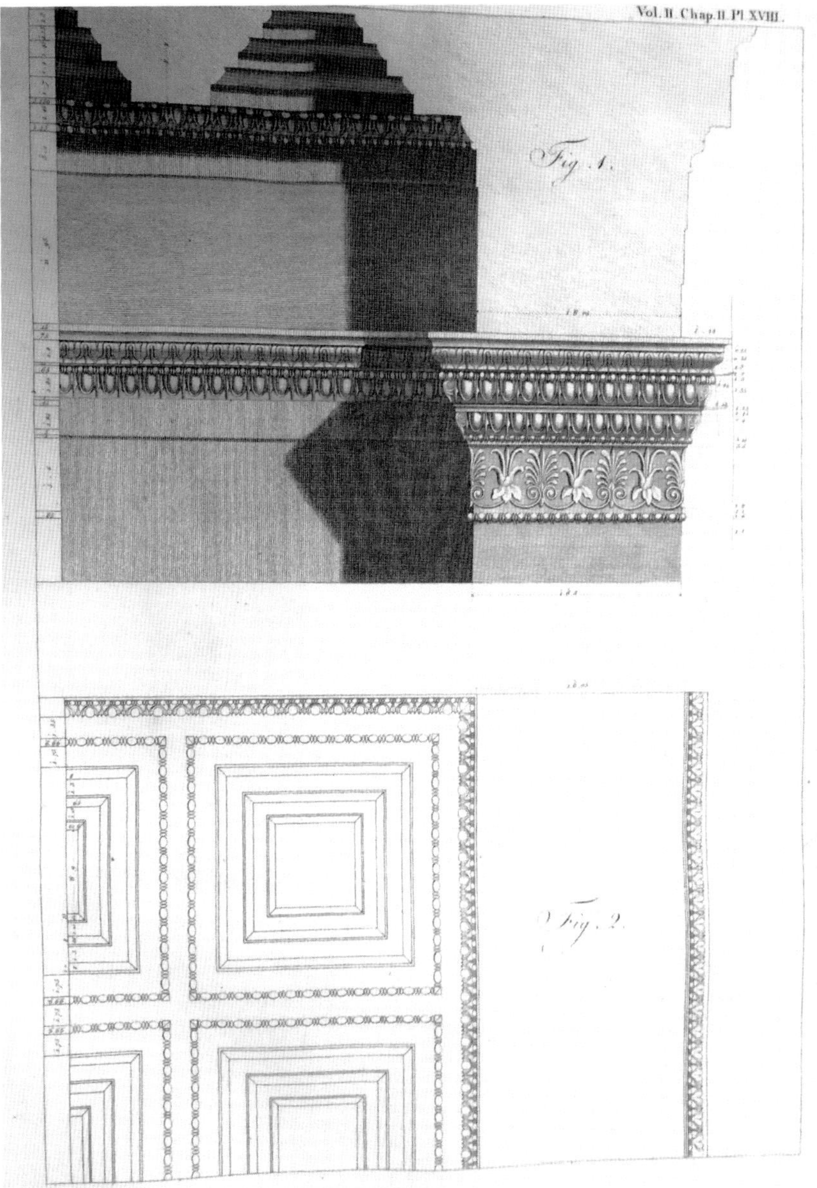

Appendix 4

Debt, subs, and Robert Stephenson

What Mackenzie didn't spell out when railing against what he saw as an eclipse of the Society's liberal ethos was what he also believed to be true, that a certain contingent of the membership wouldn't mourn the shedding of the less pecunious class of member. Unpalatable as this suggestion is, the sequel bears it out.

As Mackenzie had foreseen, over the next three decades the Society vainly struggled to reduce its debt, while member numbers declined. It took another act of huge personal generosity to rescue the situation.

In 1855 the now world-renowned Robert Stephenson agreed to be the Society's new President. He made them an offer you'd think no one could refuse. If over the next year the Society could raise half the sum owed, he would match it with a sum from his own pocket, and the debt would be cleared.

There was a condition. Annual subscription must return to one guinea.

Incredibly, from within the Committee came objections. To lower subscriptions would result in the Society's becoming "popular".

Happily the élitists were overruled. A bit behind schedule, the Society raised the sum required, subscriptions returned to their original rate, and the debt was paid off. Within a year, membership had doubled.

The Society's saviour Robert Stephenson. In 1859 he too died prematurely, bequeathing a further £7000 to the Society on condition that it wouldn't be used for any building project!

But this is jumping ahead to an era that poor Mackenzie never witnessed. In 1832, aged 54, he died in Newcastle's first cholera outbreak.

Acknowledgments

Warmest appreciation to all the Lit & Phil staff for cheerfully locating various unwieldy volumes and even heaving some of them on to the scanner. This book couldn't have happened without you.

Also huge thanks to Paul Gailiunas for knowing the best volumes to investigate and for proof-reading and photographic assistance, to Laura Wills for her patient tuition in laptop graphics, to Shima and Nick Banks for design tips, to Alison Gunning and Kay Easson for reassuring support and encouragement, and to all the friends who sympathetically responded when their ears were bent.

Thanks to the City Library for tracking down map materials and permitting their use.

And very grateful thanks to Michael Chaplin for reading the draft and writing his foreword.

The lockdowns of 2020 and 2021 are useful scapegoats to blame for sundry shortcomings; but they also have to be thanked for making me get to grips with the project in the first place.

Published Works Consulted

Scene-setting/Ancient Names

Bourne, Henry. *The history of Newcastle upon Tyne; or, The ancient and present state of that town.* Newcastle: John White, 1736.

Brand, John. *History and Antiquities of the town and county of the town of Newcastle-upon-Tyne.* London: White, 1789.

Hodgson, John. *History of Northumberland.* Part III, vol. III (Great Pipe Roll). Newcastle: Blackwell and Falconar, 1835.

Oliver, A.M. "The Baronies of Bolbec". Archaeologia Aeliana 3 vol. XXI, 1924. 142-154

Walker, Robin Fulton. *The Origins of Newcastle upon Tyne.* Newcastle: Thorne's Students' Bookshop Ltd, 1976.

Welford, Richard, ed. *History of Newcastle and Gateshead in the 14th and 15th centuries.* London: Scott, 1883.

Westmorland House and Westmorland Place

Bourne, Henry. *The history of Newcastle upon Tyne; or, The ancient and present state of that town.* Newcastle: John White, 1736.

Heslop, Richard Oliver. *Hundred and fifteenth year's Report of the Literary and Philosophical Society, Appendix G.* Newcastle: Andrew Reid & Co. Ltd, 1908. 19-22

The Monthly Chronicle of North Country Lore and Legend. vol. 2, 1888. Newcastle: Walter Scott. 406

Welford, Richard. "Westmoreland Place, Newcastle". Archaeologia Aeliana 2, vol. XIX, 1898. 223-242

Des Res

Frostick, Raymond. "James Corbridge and his Plan of Newcastle upon Tyne 1723". Archaeologia Aeliana 5 vol. 32, 2003. 171-178

Grundy, John, and Grace McCombie. Pevsner, Nikolaus. *The Buildings of England: Northumberland.* 2nd rev. ed. London: Penguin, 1992.

Heslop, D.H, B. Jobling and G. McCombie. *Alderman Fenwick's House.* Buildings of Newcastle 3. Newcastle: The Society of Antiquaries of Newcastle upon Tyne, 2001.

Laws, A.R. *Schola Novocastriensis: a biographical history of the Royal Free Grammar School of Newcastle upon Tyne.* vol. 1. Newcastle: Northumberland Press, 1925.

Philosophical Society

Barnes, Peter. "Formal Education in Manchester from 1421: The Lit & Phil as Catalyst". Manchester Memoirs vol. 150, 20011-2012. 1-15

Fitzpatrick, Martin. "Literary and philosophical societies". *An Oxford Companion to the Romantic Age: British Culture 1776-1832.* Gen. ed. Iain McCalman. Oxford, 1999.

1822-1825

Collard, William, and M. Ross. *Architectural and Picturesque Views in Newcastle-upon-Tyne; comprising Accurate Delineations of the Various Splendid Improvements which have recently been effected.* Newcastle: Collard and Ross, 1841.

Faulkner, Thomas, and Andrew Greg. *John Dobson: Architect of the North East.* Newcastle: Tyne Bridge Publishing, 2001.

Greg, Andrew. "The Building and its Architect". *Lit & Phil Bicentenary Lectures 1993,* Newcastle: The Literary and Philosophical Society of Newcastle upon Tyne, 1994. 27-47

Mackenzie, Eneas. *A Descriptive and Historical Account of the Town and County of Newcastle upon Tyne.* Newcastle: Mackenzie and Dent, 1827. 461-486

Parish, Charles. *The History of the Lit & Phil, vol II.* Newcastle: The Literary and Philosophical Society of Newcastle upon Tyne, 1990.

Stuart, James, and Nicholas Revett. *Antiquities of Athens.* 5 vols. London: Haberkorn, 1762-1830.

Watson, Robert Spence. *The History of the Literary and Philosophical Society of Newcastle-upon-Tyne (1793-1896).* London: Walter Scott, 1897.

Maps

1723: James Corbridge, *An Actual Survey of Newcastle Upon Tyne.*

1736: Henry Bourne, *A Plan of Newcastle upon Tyne,* Op. Cit.

1746: Isaac Thompson, *Plan of Newcastle upon Tyne.* (City Library)

1770: Charles Hutton, *A Plan of Newcastle upon Tyne and Gateshead.*

1827: John Wood, "Plan of Newcastle upon Tyne and Gateshead". In *Town Atlas of Northumberland and Durham by John Wood 1820-1827.* Newcastle: Frank Graham, 1991.

1828: C. & J. Greenwood, *Map of the County of Northumberland.*

1830: Thomas Oliver, *Plan of Newcastle upon Tyne and the Borough of Gateshead.*

1830: Thomas Oliver, Reduced plan of the above, *"shewing projected improvements"*. (City Library)

Illustrations

Archaeologia Aeliana 1 vol. III 1844. (View of Newcastle c.1545)

Brand, John. Op.Cit. (Assembly Rooms 1776)

Bruce, John Collingwood. *The Roman Wall* 1851. (Roman bridge and castrum: John Storey's etching of drawing by T.B.Richardson)

Bruce, John Collingwood. *The Bayeux Tapestry Elucidated* 1856. (Norman landing before Hastings)

Collard, William. Op.Cit. (Library interior; Library of the Literary and Philosophical Society)

Fox, George Townshend. *Synopsis of the Newcastle Museum 1827*. (Mummy by James Ramsay)

Mackenzie, Eneas. *An Historical, Topographical, and Descriptive View of the County of Northumberland*. Newcastle: Mackenzie and Dent, 1825. (Moot Hall)

Mackenzie, Op.Cit. 1827. (Dispensary; The New Library; Eneas Mackenzie)

Mackenzie 1827, unique edition c1880 illustrated by Dodd and Gompert. In Lit & Phil. (Intended Library Building; HRH the Duke of Sussex)

Richardson, M.A. *The Local Historian's Table Book (The Borderer's Table Book); or Gatherings of the local history and romance of the English and Scottish border*, vols. iii and v. Newcastle: Bohn, 1846. (Frontispiece; Whitefriars' Postern 1600; Westgate Street 1820; Westmorland Place 1826)

Richardson, T.M. *Memorials of Old Newcastle-upon-Tyne*. Newcastle: 1880. (Remains of Nevil Tower; Westmorland Place 1837)

Unpublished Works Consulted (Lit & Phil Collections)

The Hedley Papers: Reports, Papers and Catalogues of the Lit & Phil vol. 10; 1822.

The Fenwick Papers vol. 3; 1812-1824.

Annual Reports and miscellaneous Papers 1793-1833. vol. 13

Reports etc 1820-1824; 1825-1827.

Books of Letters vol. 1

Annual Reports 1821-27.

Committee minutes 1822.

Plans, illustrations, newspaper cuttings etc. from the above.

Headings

Headings in apostrophes have been gratefully netted from contemporary commentaries, largely of Eneas Mackenzie but also of Metcalf Ross et al.

Printed by Biddles Books Ltd, King's Lynn, Norfolk